The Modern American Novel 1914–1945

A Critical History

Twayne's Critical History of the Novel

Herbert Sussman, Series Editor
Northeastern University

The Modern American Novel 1914–1945

A Critical History

Linda Wagner-Martin
University of North Carolina at Chapel Hill

Twayne Publishers
A Division of G. K. Hall & Co. • *Boston*

The Modern American Novel, 1914–1945: A Critical History
Linda Wagner-Martin

Copyright 1990 by Linda Wagner-Martin
All rights reserved,
Published by Twayne Publishers
A Division of G. K. Hall & Co.
70 Lincoln Street
Boston, Massachusetts 02111

Copyediting supervised by Barbara Sutton.
Book production by Gabrielle B. McDonald.

Typeset in 10 pt. Palatino
by Huron Valley Graphics, Inc., Ann Arbor, Michigan.

Printed on permanent/durable acid-free paper
and bound in the United States of America.

Library of Congress Cataloging-in-Publication Data

Wagner–Martin, Linda.
    The modern American novel, 1914–1945 : a critical history / Linda
Wagner-Martin.
        p.   cm.—(Twayne's critical history of the novel)
    Bibliography: p.
    Includes index.
    ISBN 0-8057-7851-9 (alk. paper)
        1. American fiction—20th century—History and criticism.
    2. American fiction—Chronology.   3. American fiction—Bibliography.
    I. Title.   II. Series.
    PS379.W27   1989
    813'.5209—dc20

                                                                89-15515
                                                                CIP

For Andrea, Tom, and Doug

Contents

Preface

As the twentieth century approaches its end, literary historians and critics of American modernism have the advantage of distance. The patterns that once seemed dominant—given various cycles of academic enthusiasm—have taken on fainter outlines, while the configurations of new patterns have grown sharper. The landscape of American modernism looks different to observers now than it did in 1950 or 1960. Its general effect is richer, busier. It appears to be a canvas marked with pastels as well as intense primary colors, filled with both impressionistic sketches and primitive outlines. And the canvas itself has widened so that it can include rather than limit, can draw from hundreds of important literary works instead of a handful.

Essential additions to texts available, as well as changes in critical attitudes, have fed into current theoretical strategies that would have seemed revolutionary at the middle of this century. Now that readers can experience, again, some of what was really being written and read in the years of World War I and World War II, and between them, it is difficult to accept summary descriptions of modernism as a wasteland, depicting life under seige, bereft of fulfillment or joy. In fact, a great amount of writing published from 1910 to 1945 celebrated life and challenged the apathy of disillusionment.

Changes in attitude are never easy, and those that have occurred recently within the literary community are far reaching. To say that the canon has changed because women's or minority writers' books have been added to those previously taught—those written by white males—is oversimplification. Learning to read modernist fiction for what it is—rather than for what we had sometimes been taught that it was—was and is difficult, although the work of Nina Baym and Annette Kolodny has helped immensely. Baym's distinguishing traditional (male-identified) patterns in both American literature and its criticism made clearer the rationale for critics of modernist literature privileging certain fictions.[1] Kolodny's pointing out that the literary profession creates hierarchies of value—so that some books are more acceptable than others ("better," more worthy of discussion)—added new terminology to our often unvoiced opinions.[2] New critical terms, whether from American, British, or French feminist critics or black and other ethnic observers, gave us further means of expressing ideas about books we had been accustomed to discussing in limited and traditional ways. Not only were we gaining access to new fictions; we were reading familiar texts from new critical perspectives. By the early 1980s, the (wide) world of modernist literature mattered once again.

This study attempts to bring the sense of rich innovation back into our concept of modernism by naming, first in the Chronology and then in the body of the text, the many works that were influential in their time, although they may be less than household words today. To illustrate the wealth of good writing published during this time, one chapter discusses fiction from 1925, a single year burgeoning with a variety of provocative novels. Another method used here is to juxtapose expected books with those less anticipated: Hemingway's 1926 novel, *The Sun Also Rises*, a touchstone of modernism, is discussed alongside Nella Larsen's 1928 novel, *Quicksand*. Larsen's narrative of a black woman's life, a quest novel in which the protagonist goes abroad to find a truer sense of herself, both extends and counters Hemingway's story of American and British expatriates, searching for fulfillment in Paris and Spain during the same time period. Similarly, H.D.'s novel *HERmione* is discussed in tandem with John Dos Passos's *U.S.A.* trilogy, and Gertrude Stein's *Three Lives* with work by Sherwood Anderson.

Another strategy of this book is to redefine concepts. In a discussion of expatriation with the Harlem Renaissance, I suggest that the writers' need to "revolt from the village," to escape confining American middle-class culture, was met by both physical travel to Europe and the imaginative exploration of the Afro-American culture possible during the years when "Harlem was in vogue." An early chapter of the study also emphasizes the centrality of fiction by Edith Wharton, Ellen Glasgow, and Willa Cather as separate from—and probably more influential to modernist fiction than—the writing of Stephen Crane and Frank Norris.

Much of this redefining is meant to allow readers to erase hard categorical lines, to combine separate bins and boxes of writing so that the glorious, if chaotic, masses of language—which comprised modernist writing—can have the same impact on today's reader that it had on readers of the time. To that end, one early chapter sets the development of modernist prose fiction in the context of these same writers' experiments with poetry. Because during the years of modernism writers wrote in all genres, were in some ways much less self-conscious about external definitions of the writer, our later critical tendency to separate story from poem, fiction from drama, memoir from all, has led to false or at least misleading perspectives.

The last chapters of this book continue the discussion of the familiar modernist work—most of it written during the 1920s or earlier—into the 1930s and the 1940s. The chapter on literature of the 1930s emphasizes the role women writers and black writers played in the new consciousness of community as theme, illustrated through discussion of the "lost" work of Meridel Le Sueur. Fiction by William Faulkner, which is often isolated from other texts of the 1930s, also benefits from being studied in such a context. And just as the chapter on writing during the 1930s does, the chapter on the 1940s stresses the continuance of modernist strategies and techniques even in later texts that might appear to be differently conceived.

My study is clearly—and, I hope, convincingly—revisionist. It attempts to give coherent shape to a period that was flooded with memorable, skillful, and pertinent fiction, recognizing that coherence need not be exclusive or lifeless. During the 1980s, we have been aided in these kinds of redefinitions because of wide attention to issues of "canon" and "knowledge as prescribed lists," issues that during the 1960s might have been relegated to courses in black studies or women's studies. In the 1980s, as in the 1920s, the reader-text relationship has been meaningful and productive; the variousness of fiction is matched only by great variety in readers' perspectives. This book is intended to be an open-ended contribution to that ongoing development of the canon, an affirmation that literary history of the best kind is evolving rather than static.

Linda Wagner-Martin

Chapel Hill, North Carolina

Chronology

This chronology gives some sense of the intense activity in both England and America during these years. Novels, collections of short fiction, and nonfiction works appear in the first section of each listing by year, followed by titles of collections of poetry and plays, and then by magazine listings. Deaths of significant writers are mentioned last. Not every work by each author appears; the sampling can be augmented by titles in the Bibliography.

1909   Gertrude Stein, *Three Lives*. Jack London, *Martin Eden*. Ezra Pound, *Personae*. Sarah Orne Jewett dies.

1910   Edwin Arlington Robinson, *Town down the River*. Hamlin Garland, *Other Main-Travelled Roads*.

1911   Edith Wharton, *Ethan Frome*. Theodore Dreiser, *Jennie Gerhard*. W. E. B. Du Bois, *The Quest of the Silver Fleece*. *Masses* begun.

1912   James Weldon Johnson, *Autobiography of an Ex-Colored Man*. Mary Antin, *Promised Land*. Amy Lowell, *A Dome of Many-Colored Glass*. Futurist Exhibition. *Poetry* begun.

1913   Willa Cather, *O Pioneers!* Edith Wharton, *The Custom of the Country*. Ellen Glasgow, *Virginia*. Robert Frost, *A Boy's Will*. Paul Laurence Dunbar, *Complete Poems*. Freud's *Interpretation of Dreams* translated into English. The Amory Show. *Smart Set* begun.

1914   James Joyce, *Dubliners*. Gertrude Stein, *Tender Buttons*. Robert Frost, *North of Boston*. Emily Dickinson, *The Single Hound* (first publication). Vorticism. *Blast*, *New Republic*, and *Little Review* begun.

1915   Willa Cather, *The Song of the Lark*. Edgar Lee Masters, *Spoon River Anthology*. Ezra Pound, *Cathay*; *Some Imagist Poets, 1915–1917*. Provincetown Players and Washington Square Players founded.

1916   James Joyce, *A Portrait of the Artist as a Young Man.* Ring
       Lardner, *You Know Me, Al.* Carl Sandburg, *Chicago Poems.*
       H.D., *Sea Garden.* Susan Glaspell, *Trifles.* Carl Jung, *Psychol-
       ogy of the Unconscious.* John Dewey, *Democracy and Education.*
       Seven Arts begun; Henry James and Jack London die.

1917   Edith Wharton, *Summer.* Hamlin Garland, *A Son of the Mid-
       dle Border.* Sara Teasdale, *Love Songs.* T. S. Eliot, *Prufrock and
       Other Poems.* Edna St. Vincent Millay, *Renascence.* William
       Carlos Williams, *Al Que Quiere!* William Butler Yeats, *The
       Wild Swans at Coole. Ulysses* published in *Little Review.*

1918   Willa Cather, *My Ántonia.* Henry Adams, *The Education of
       Henry Adams.* Lola Ridge, *The Ghetto.* D. H. Lawrence, *New
       Poems.* Eugene O'Neill, *Moon of the Caribees. Dial* begun.

1919   Sherwood Anderson, *Winesburg, Ohio.* James Branch Cabell,
       Jurgen. H. L. Mencken, *American Language.* John Reed, *Ten
       Days That Shook the World.* Prohibition enacted.

1920   Edith Wharton, *The Age of Innocence.* F. Scott Fitzgerald, *This
       Side of Paradise.* Sinclair Lewis, *Main Street.* Anzia Yezierska,
       Hungry Hearts. D. H. Lawrence, *Women in Love.* Ezra Pound,
       Hugh Selwyn Mauberley. Eugene O'Neill, *Emperor Jones.*

1921   John Dos Passos, *Three Soldiers.* Sherwood Anderson, *The
       Triumph of the Egg.* Evelyn Scott, *The Narrow House.* Elinor
       Wylie, *Nets to Catch the Wind.* Marianne Moore, *Poems.* Wil-
       liam Carlos Williams, *Sour Grapes.* Susan Glaspell, *The Verge.*

1922   F. Scott Fitzgerald, *The Beautiful and Damned.* Edith Whar-
       ton, *Glimpses of the Moon.* James Joyce, *Ulysses.* Willa Cather,
       One of Ours. Sinclair Lewis, *Babbitt.* e. e. cummings, *The
       Enormous Room.* Claude McKay, *Harlem Shadows.* T. S. Eliot,
       The Waste Land.

1923   Willa Cather, *A Lost Lady.* Elinor Wylie, *Jennifer Lorn.* Sher-
       wood Anderson, *Many Marriages.* Jean Toomer, *Cane.* Fan-
       nie Hurst, *Lummox.* Edith Summers Kelley, *Weeds.* Djuna
       Barnes, *A Book.* Wallace Stevens, *Harmonium.* e. e. cum-
       mings, *Tulips and Chimneys.* John Howard Lawson, *Roger
       Bloomer.* Elmer Rice, *The Adding Machine. Opportunity* begun.

1924   Herman Melville, *Billy Budd* (first publication). Ernest Hem-
       ingway, *in our time.* Jessie Redmon Fauset, *There is Confusion.*
       Edna Ferber, *So Big.* T. E. Hulme, *Speculations.* Emily Dickinson,

Complete Poems (first publication). Eugene O'Neill, *Desire under the Elms* and *All God's Chillun*. *American Mercury* begun.

1925 F. Scott Fitzgerald, *The Great Gatsby*. Willa Cather, *The Professor's House*. Ernest Hemingway, *In Our Time*. John Dos Passos, *Manhattan Transfer*. Gertrude Stein, *The Making of Americans*. Sinclair Lewis, *Arrowsmith*. Theodore Dreiser, *An American Tragedy*. Ellen Glasgow, *Barren Ground*. Edith Wharton's *A Mother's Recompense*. Anzia Yezierska, *Bread Givers*. Sherwood Anderson, *Dark Laughter*. William Carlos Williams, *In the American Grain*. Alain Locke, ed., *The New Negro: An Interpretation*. DuBose Heyward, *Porgy*. John Howard Lawson, *Processional*. Countee Cullen, *Color*. Robinson Jeffers, *Tamar* and *Roan Stallion*. H.D., *Collected Poems*. Amy Lowell dies.

1926 H.D., *Palimpsest*. Ernest Hemingway, *The Sun Also Rises* and *The Torrents of Spring*. William Faulkner, *Soldiers' Pay*. Elizabeth Madox Roberts, *The Time of Man*. Carl Van Vechten, *Nigger Heaven*. Dorothy Parker, *Enough Rope*. Langston Hughes, *The Weary Blues*. Hart Crane, *White Buildings*.

1927 Willa Cather, *Death Comes for the Archbishop*. Conrad Aiken, *Blue Voyage*. Ernest Hemingway, *Men without Women*. Mourning Dove, *Cogewea the Half-Blood*. O. E. Rolvaag, *Giants in the Earth*. Glenway Wescott, *The Grandmothers*. Carl Sandburg, *American Songbag*. Langston Hughes, *Fine Clothes to the Jew*. e. e. cummings, *him*. Alain Locke, ed., *Plays of Negro Life*. *Transition* and *American Caravan* begun.

1928 Nella Larsen, *Quicksand*. William Faulkner, *Mosquitoes*. D. H. Lawrence, *Lady Chatterley*. Claude McKay, *Home to Harlem*. W. E. B. Du Bois, *Dark Princess*. Jessie Redmon Fauset, *Plum Bun*. William Carlos Williams, *A Voyage to Pagany*. Stephen Vincent Benet, *John Brown's Body*. Robert Frost, *West-Running Brook*. Allen Tate, *Mr. Pope and Other Poems*. *American Literature* founded; Elinor Wylie dies.

1929 William Faulkner, *Sartoris* and *The Sound and the Fury*. Thomas Wolfe, *Look Homeward, Angel*. Ernest Hemingway, *A Farewell to Arms*. Langston Hughes, *Not Without Laughter*. Claude McKay, *Banjo*. Oliver La Farge, *Laughing Boy*. Agnes Smedley, *Daughter of Earth*. Nella Larsen, *Passing*. Louise Bogan, *Dark Summer*.

1930   William Faulkner, *As I Lay Dying*. John Dos Passos, *The 42nd Parallel*. Katherine Anne Porter, *Flowering Judas*. Dashiell Hammett, *The Maltese Falcon*. T. S. Eliot, *Ash Wednesday*. Hart Crane, *The Bridge*. Susan Glaspell, *Alison's House*. Southern Agrarians and Fugitives, *I'll Take My Stand*. Sinclair Lewis is the first American to win the Nobel Prize for Literature; D. H. Lawrence dies.

1931   Thomas Stribling, *The Forge*. Caroline Gordon, *Penhally*. Pearl Buck, *The Good Earth*. William Faulkner, *Sanctuary*. Arna Bontemps, *God Sends Sunday*. Fannie Hurst, *Back Street*. Emma Goldman, *Living My Life*. Eugene O'Neill, *Mourning Becomes Electra*. Vachel Lindsay dies.

1932   John Dos Passos, *1919*. Erskine Caldwell, *Tobacco Road*. James T. Farrell, *Young Lonigan*. Ellen Glasgow, *The Sheltered Life*. William Faulkner, *Light in August*. Ernest Hemingway, *Death in the Afternoon*. Zelda Fitzgerald, *Save Me the Waltz*. Kay Boyle, *The Wedding Day*. Countee Cullen, *One Way to Heaven*. Claude McKay, *Gingertown*. Archibald MacLeish, *Conquistador*. Hart Crane dies.

1933   Nathanael West, *Miss Lonelyhearts*. Gertrude Stein, *The Autobiography of Alice B. Toklas*. Claude McKay, *Banana Bottom*. Eugene O'Neill, *Ah, Wilderness!* Hart Crane, *Collected Poems*. James Weldon Johnson, *Along the Way*. Sterling A. Brown, *Southern Road*. Sara Teasdale dies.

1934   F. Scott Fitzgerald, *Tender Is the Night*. Henry Miller, *Tropic of Cancer*. William Saroyan, *The Daring Young Man on the Flying Trapeze*. Zora Neale Hurston, *Jonah's Gourd Vine*. Tess Slesinger, *The Unpossessed*. Ruth Suckow, *The Folks*. Josephine Herbst, *The Executioner Waits*. Josephine Johnson, *Now in November*. Henry Roth, *Call It Sleep*. Edna St. Vincent Millay, *Wine from These Grapes*. Lillian Hellman, *The Children's Hour*.

1935   William Faulkner, *Pylon*. John Steinbeck, *Tortilla Flat*. Albert Maltz, *Black Pit*. Ellen Glasgow, *Vein of Iron*. Ernest Hemingway, *Green Hills of Africa*. Zora Neale Hurston, *Mules and Men*. Wallace Stevens, *Ideas of Order*. e. e. cummings, *No Thanks*. Ezra Pound, *Make It New* and *Jefferson and/or Mussolini*. Muriel Rukeyser, *Theory of Flight*. Robert Penn Warren, *Thirty-six Poems*. Langston Hughes, *Mulatto*. Clifford Odets,

Waiting for Lefty and *Awake and Sing*. Maxwell Anderson, *Winterset*. T. S. Eliot, *Murder in the Cathedral*. Federal Writers' Project, 1935–39.

1936 John Dos Passos, *The Big Money*. Arna Bontemps, *Black Thunder*. William Faulkner, *Absalom, Absalom!* John Steinbeck, *In Dubious Battle*. Meridel Le Sueur, *The Girl*. Djuna Barnes, *Nightwood*. Margaret Mitchell, *Gone with the Wind*. Harriette Arnow, *Mountain Path*. James M. Cain, *The Postman Always Rings Twice*. Robert Frost, *A Further Range*. Carl Sandburg, *The People, Yes*. Eugene O'Neill receives Nobel Prize for Literature; Federal Theatre Project begun.

1937 Ernest Hemingway, *To Have and Have Not*. John Steinbeck, *The Red Pony* and *Of Mice and Men*. John Marquand, *The Late George Apley*. Zora Neale Hurston, *Their Eyes Were Watching God*. William Carlos Williams, *White Mule*. Younghill Kang, *East Goes West*. Lin Yutang, *My Country and My People*. Gertrude Stein, *Everybody's Autobiography*. Erskine Caldwell and Margaret Bourke White, *You Have Seen Their Faces*. Wallace Stevens, *The Man with the Blue Guitar*. Edith Wharton dies.

1938 William Faulkner, *The Unvanquished*. John Dos Passos, *U.S.A*. Richard Wright, *Uncle Tom's Children*. Delmore Schwartz, *In Dreams Begin Responsibilities*. e. e. cummings, *Collected Poems*. Laura Riding, *Collected Poems*. Robert Sherwood, *Abe Lincoln in Illinois*. Ernest Hemingway, *The Fifth Column; The Spanish Earth* (Spanish Civil War film). Pearl Buck receives Nobel Prize for Literature; Thomas Wolfe dies.

1939 John Steinbeck, *The Grapes of Wrath*. William Faulkner, *The Wild Palms*. Katherine Anne Porter, *Pale Horse, Pale Rider*. Anaïs Nin, *The Winter of Artifice*. Nathanael West, *The Day of the Locust*. Pietro Di Donato, *Christ in Concrete*. Henry Miller, *Tropic of Capricorn*. James Joyce, *Finnegans Wake*. Ezra Pound, *The ABC of Economics*. Robert Penn Warren, *Night Rider*. T. S. Eliot, *The Family Reunion*. Lillian Hellman, *The Little Foxes*. Dorothea Lange and Paul S. Taylor, *An American Exodus*. William Butler Yeats dies.

1940 Richard Wright, *Native Son*. Carson McCullers, *The Heart Is a Lonely Hunter*. Thomas Wolfe, *You Can't Go Home Again*. Ernest Hemingway, *For Whom the Bell Tolls*. William Faulkner, *The Hamlet*. Glenway Wescott, *Pilgrim Hawk*. Martha Gellhorn, *A Stricken Field*. Albert Halper, *Sons of the Fathers*. Janet Flanner, *An American in Paris*. Langston Hughes, *The Big Sea*. Ezra Pound, *The Cantos*. Eugene O'Neill, *Long Day's Journey into Night*. Hamlin Garland, Emma Goldman, Nathanael West, and F. Scott Fitzgerald die.

1941   Carson McCullers, *Reflections in a Golden Eye*. Eudora Welty, *A Curtain of Green*. Caroline Gordon, *Green Centuries*. Gertrude Stein, *Ida*. F. Scott Fitzgerald, *The Last Tycoon*. James Agee and Walker Evans, *Let Us Now Praise Famous Men*. Marianne Moore, *What Are Years?* Theodore Roethke, *Open House*. Lillian Hellman, *Watch on the Rhine*. Sherwood Anderson dies.

1942   Eudora Welty, *The Robber Bridegroom*. William Faulkner, *Go Down, Moses*. Albert Camus, *L'Etranger*. Kay Boyle, *Primer for Combat*. John Steinbeck, *The Moon Is Down*. Kenneth Burke, *The White Oxen*. Mary McCarthy, *The Company She Keeps*. Nelson Algren, *Never Come Morning*. Ruth Suckow, *New Hope*. Wright Morris, *My Uncle Dudley*. James Gould Cozzens, *The Just and the Unjust*. Wallace Stevens, *Notes toward a Supreme Fiction*. Robert Frost, *A Witness Tree*. Muriel Rukeyser, *Wake Island*. Margaret Walker, *For My People*. Thornton Wilder, *The Skin of Our Teeth*.

1943   John Dos Passos, *Number One*. Ira Wolfert, *Tucker's People*. Wallace Stegner, *The Big Rock Candy Mountain*. Carlos Bulosan, *The Voice of Bataan*. Ayn Rand, *The Fountainhead*. T. S. Eliot, *Four Quartets*. Kenneth Fearing, *Afternoon of a Pawnbroker*. Robert Penn Warren, *At Heaven's Gate*.

1944   Caroline Gordon, *The Women on the Porch*. Kay Boyle, *Avalanche*. Harry Brown, *A Walk in the Sun*. Jean Stafford, *Boston Adventure*. Saul Bellow, *Dangling Man*. John Steinbeck, *Cannery Row*. Anaïs Nin, *Under a Glass Bell*. John Hersey, *A Bell for Adano*. Lillian Smith, *Strange Fruit*. Carlos Bulosan, *Laughter of My Father*. Lillian Hellman, *The Searching Wind*. William Carlos Williams, *The Wedge*. Robert Lowell, *Land of Unlikeness*.

1945   Chester Himes, *If He Hollers Let Him Go*. Eudora Welty, *Delta Wedding*. Richard Wright, *Black Boy*. Gertrude Stein, *Wars I*

Have Seen. F. Scott Fitzgerald, *The Crack-Up.* H.D., *Tribute to the Angels* and *The Walls Do Not Fall.* Robert Frost, *A Masque of Reason.* Gwendolyn Brooks, *A Street in Bronzeville.* Tennessee Williams, *The Glass Menagerie.* Theodore Dreiser and Ellen Glasgow die.

1

The Question of Modernism

Modernism was startling in its innovation and dramatic in its concision, as it spoke for a "wasteland" view of existence. What hope or satisfaction could have been found in the Victorian concepts of order and religion had been devastated by industrialization and its resulting economic and social changes. International dissension would culminate in World War I (Virginia Woolf would later write, flippantly, "on or about December, 1910, human character changed").[1] American and European society had shifted from the belief in Browning's comforting refrain, "God's in his heaven. All's right with the world," to a decidedly irreverent questioning of all known experience. If there was no preordained order, why live a moral life? If there was no God, why try to please one? And if there was no eternal reward, why not enjoy life in the present? The desire for immediate satisfactions dominated much twentieth-century thought and helped to create a new conception of time (Bergsonian durée), as well as different ideas about the way present time relates to both the future and the past. The latter relationship was to provide an important theme for modernist literature.[2]

Modernism as literary history has defined it lasted from before World War I—some would say from impressionism—to the 1940s. Maurice Beebe terms it "an international current of sensibility which dominated art and literature . . . distinguished by its formalism."[3] For Beebe, modernist writing is characterized by a mythic structure, a close attention to form and method, an ironic point of view that allows the writer to remain objective about the subject, and a solipsistic self-consciousness that the writer is creating self and time through writing. For Gaylord Leroy and Ursula Beitz, who date the movement from the last third of the nineteenth century, modernism was "marked by pessimism, with foreshadowings of the modern existential Angst. . . . We have in Modernism a shift from life to art; art becomes a substitute for life, or a refuge from it."[4] Such precise definitions—though partially accurate—quickly can become exclusionary. They suggest a pervasive uniformity, a belief that hundreds of aspiring and established writers were somehow privy to the same aesthetic and thematic ideas, which were then reflected in the same way in everything written. Such an implication is wrong. Modernism has long been synonymous with diversity, and its complex and rich assortment of texts grew from more than diverse aesthetic positions. The early twentieth century saw the rise of many new publishing firms, all eager to handle new writers. Given the immense quantity of fiction, poetry, and drama being written and published, restrictive definitions of modernism are even more misleading. They leave the reader in the quandary of knowing that of the great wealth of modernist literature, some is more "modern"— and therefore presumably "better"—than the rest. As Quentin Anderson recently wrote, "Modernism is a term open to attack in an age that questions the prevailing literary canon as too narrow and exclusive. Few writers are called Modernists, and those few have been given the status of an elite."[5] This book will discuss the traditional concepts and texts of modernism, as well as the reasons those concepts and texts are being questioned today.

Part of the difficulty of considering modernism as a movement is that so much of its rationale grew out of nineteenth-century thought. Even if it seemed as though outward regulation had given way to inner, personal choice—especially since religious belief seemed to have been eclipsed—such philosophies drew from those of Nietzsche, Hobbes, Hegel, Marx, Darwin, T. E. Hulme, F. H. Bradley, William James, Henri Bergson, and Sigmund Freud, not to mention John Dewey, Santayana, and Whitehead. Currents of materialism and pragmatism—the insistence on immediate knowledge and satisfactions—had reinforced much earlier thought. Such beliefs recognized the animal (the primitive, the sexual) in the human; they also saw that people were responsible for their acts. On the positive side, individuals were no longer trapped by birth and social stratification. Like Horatio Alger, they believed they could become whatever they chose. On the negative, the choices possible in the newly relativistic world were sometimes confusing, if not frightening.

What such immense philosophical change meant for literature was that both subject matter and form became obviously "new."

When Ezra Pound walked the streets of London wearing his scarf with its legend, "Make it new," he voiced the convictions of the young literary world. Edmund Wilson recalled that writers contemporary with him wanted to create "something in which every word, every cadence, every detail, should perform a definite function in producing an intense effect."[6] And Gorham Munson reminisced about the division between the new writers and the more traditional at a party for Edgar Lee Masters: "The younger people were as usual discussing the everlasting topic of form, the older people aired their views on anti-religion."[7]

In just a few years, writing had almost replaced religion, and readers and critics judged a writer's worth as it appeared in "the work." T. S. Eliot wrote that "the task of the artist is a task in the same sense as the making of an efficient engine or the turning of a jug or a table leg."[8] Skilled in their craft, the modernist writers knew that the chaos they faced living in the twentieth century called for distance and objectivity, laconic expression and the seeming ineptitude of common speech. The language of modernist literature was chosen not so much because it could be a way to reach the common reader but rather as a means of protecting the writers themselves from the frustration of incomplete and probably faulty knowledge, the bleak wartime landscape starred with dead bodies, and the increasingly impersonal newsreels and headlines that charted this modern age. Modernism became the literature of the expert tour de force: Gertrude Stein's *Tender Buttons,* William Faulkner's *The Sound and the Fury* and *As I Lay Dying,* John Dos Passos's *U.S.A.* So overwhelmingly new were these works, so conscious of their involved experimentation, that many modernist writers despaired of ever reaching such heights of innovation themselves. And the attainment mattered.

Perhaps more significantly than its themes, modernism's craft came to be its focal point. Readers discussed how the story was told, how the line was broken, how effects were created. Modern writing meant structural and linguistic experimentation. Just as the writer was to be the inventor, so was he or she to understand the invention that marked cubism, dada, futurism, vorticism—or, as John Dos Passos recalled, "Currents of energy seemed breaking out everywhere. . . . Americans were groggy with new things in theatre and painting and music."[9] He described this "creative tidal wave" further:

Under various tags: futurism, cubism, vorticism, modernism, most of the best work in the arts in our time has been the direct product of this explosion, that had an influence in its sphere comparable with that of the October revolution in social organization and politics and the Einstein formula in physics. Cendrars and Apollinaire, poets, were on the first cubist barricades with the group that influenced Picasso, Modigliani, Marinetti, Chagall; that profoundly influenced Maiakovsky, Meyerhold, Eisenstein; whose ideas carom through Joyce, Gertrude Stein, T. S. Eliot.[10]

Out of this creative tidal wave grew the techniques of juxtaposition, fragmented structures, plotless and open narrative—all used to portray decidedly common and usually unheroic characters. All kinds of writing centered around an image or scene that served to hold the broken pieces of text together; visually compelling, the image or scene was a pragmatic focus for its art. Literature, then, presented not some abstract idea of the pastoral but rather William Carlos Williams's red wheelbarrow; not a sense of postwar anguish but Hemingway's lonely young soldier off fishing the Big Two-Hearted River. Modernists wrote about the real, and from the tactic Williams described as "no ideas but in things," readers drew the more generalized meaning for themselves.

Modernism was both self-conscious and formalist. It used method and control of craft to reach readers, methods that included violence and shock. Many of the techniques used in this literature were borrowed from visual art, film, and poetry and signaled those other arts to the reader. In the modernists' view, literature was to be suggestive, not didactic. It was to work through indirection. It might even pretend to be unliterary, using colloquial speech rather than poetic diction or literary language.

Similarly, the modernists chose common characters and tried in describing them to achieve psychological accuracy. In this writing, characters were interesting not so much for what they did but for their motivation. F. Scott Fitzgerald's Gatsby is surely a failure, but his reasons for his life choices make him memorable. Willa Cather's Ántonia lives a remarkably placid, hard-working life, but in the eyes of the novel's narrator, it seems romantic and fulfilling. William Faulkner's Temple Drake interests the reader not for anything she does but because her portrayal is an incredibly prescient depiction of rape trauma. And because characters were to appear as live, they appeared in interaction and were drawn through dialogue and scene. Therefore the role of the author as storyteller changed dramatically; there was little obvious authorial intervention. The author shaped the narrative through selection of detail and scene, through choice of character and method—he or she did not appear in the text proper. If an author's presence was noticeable, his or her voice was the reportorial objective mode, distanced into irony.

The icon of American modernism was T. S. Eliot's *The Waste Land* (1922), a long poem that described the modern age through an apparently impersonal collage of scene, dialogue, and allusion to other examples of Western history and literature. (Eliot himself had described the poem as "a personal and wholly insignificant grouse against life . . . a piece of rhythmical grumbling,"[11] but it captured the modernist sensibility so well that it seemed to express the culture of the time.) The poem was structured as a montage of separate scenes (the speaker in the poem says near its end, "These fragments I have shored against my ruin," explaining the method as if it were theme), and it evoked the sense of journey. Archetypal in many of its themes, *The Waste Land* echoed what was to be known as the mythic method, used to the fullest extent in James Joyce's 1922 novel, *Ulysses*. Much modernist literature traced a search or journey, drew on life-giving water or sunlight and darkness, and made clear the importance of Freud, Jung, Frazier, and other accounts of both archetypes and myth.

In Eliot's *The Waste Land*, the Fisher King attempts to save his country from drought, searching for water to transform the wasted land into a fruitful one. The distancing of grief and anger that the poet conveyed illustrated Eliot's notion of the objective correlative perfectly: the artist was to choose an object, a concrete image, to convey feelings rather than expressing those feelings directly to the reader. Irony was the mode for most of the poem, and the numerous allusions reinforced the idea that language had become code. Only readers who had experienced the disillusion that modernist texts described could be accurate readers. What resulted from the modernists' use of irony, highly innovative forms, and fragmentation was an art that some readers could not decipher on their own. Modernist texts accordingly became the subjects of close, careful explication, and New Criticism was eventually born.

Modern writing was also almost completely, sometimes overwhelmingly, serious. Angst at the ultimate recognition—the meaninglessness of human life, either learned through the failure of religious belief or the destruction of war—pervaded most literature from the time of the Great War through the 1920s and into the 1930s. With the end of peace and the onset of a second world war even more devastating than the first, readers' temperaments changed, and they searched increasingly for humor. There had been little of that in modernist writing, and when it had appeared, readers usually overlooked it.

Because the literature of modernism struggled to meet so many caveats, a great many themes never appeared. War—complete with violence and brutality—seemed appropriate. That subject could be treated with irony, could be viewed seriously, could be the topic for experimental techniques, and writers as diverse as John Dos Passos, e. e. cummings, Ernest Hemingway, William Faulkner, Willa Cather, and Edith Wharton wrote well about its waste. The pervasive American theme of the young man coming to maturity and wisdom through adolescence—the classic bildungsroman—dominated many novels, and the depiction of the particularly modern American culture, with its capitalistic economic and personal ideals, accounted for many modernist texts. But seldom in the canon of this literature are there novels about the fulfillment of family life, positive relationships among sisters or among mothers and children, same-sex friendships for women, or a woman's capacity to find satisfaction in life. When writers did create bildungsromane about women characters, as Cather did in *The Song of the Lark*, Glasgow did in *Virginia* and *Life and Gabriella*, Wharton did in *Glimpses of the Moon* and its prototype, *The House of Mirth*, as well as *Summer* and *The Reef*, those characters often failed to reach success or happiness. And frequently, in fiction that seemed to be about men and women in relationships, the author's focus was on the male character; women repeatedly took second billing. Women in modernist fiction were often people who proved the merits or demerits of the male characters rather than being important in their own right.

While many readers and critics have considered modernist writing as one apex of American literary expression, critics more recently have challenged its eminence partly on the grounds that it failed to present a range of human emotions and experience germane to all readers, regardless of education, gender, race, or religious or political persuasion. Collectively much modern literature has emphasized male experience and belief, and it has consistently privileged writing because of its narrative difficulty. But in fact, after fifty years of critical study of the work that was produced during modernism, some critics now contend that modernism was both elitist and reductive in that it ignored whole segments of experience and therefore of readers. What was once a canon of writing called "modernist" has become a topic of sharp controversy. Andrew Ross, in *The Failure of Modernism*, sees faults between the writers' avowed objectivity and their actual deep involvement, their true subjectivity.[12] Sandra M. Gilbert and Susan Gubar point to the importance of the many women writers from the turn of the century through World War II and claim that the "New Woman" issue was as important a thematic interest as World War I or alienation—perhaps leading men who wrote to create misogynist or misleading portraits of women characters.[13] Shari Benstock challenges the whole concept of modernism as it has been defined, drawing on both Marxist and feminist theory. She describes the results of new approaches to cultural history and the inclusion of the important expatriate women and their communities in the context of modernism. She writes in *Women of the Left Bank*,

Feminist criticism directed toward rediscovery and reevaluation of the work of women writers has already altered our view of Modernism as a literary movement. It has testified to female experience in the social and intellectual settings of modern history and has examined the modes of entrapment, betrayal, and exclusion suffered by women in the first decades of the twentieth century. It has exposed the absence of commentary on women's contributions to Modernism and has rewritten the history of individual women's lives and works within the Modernist context. . . . Once women Modernists are placed beside their male colleagues, the hegemony of masculine heterosexual values that have for so long underwritten our definitions of Modernism is put into question. Modernism may then be seen to be a far more eclectic and richly diverse literary movement than has previously been assumed.[14]

As a result of these new conceptions of the period, earlier accounts of modernism seem incomplete, and the deference readers once paid to Ernest Hemingway, William Faulkner, and James Joyce has diminished under the charge that their concentration on certain kinds of experience was not liberating but myopic and that their inward-looking focus was more narrowing than the vision of writers who chose to describe wider canvases. It also seems clear that reading only the canonized modernist texts gives the reader the sense of Prufrockian debilitation, of cynical austerity that has no vitality, energy, or even feeling—traits that certainly belong in a portrait of an expanding America at the turn of the century.[15]

Accordingly, this study will include discussion of a number of writers and texts, among them some that may have been overlooked in the recent past. At its best, the age of modernism was a busy, even chaotic, period of literary activity that had a wide range of successes and failures. It begins with some transitional figures, the writers at the turn of this century who were being read and talked about, who were incipient modernists, although they might more readily be called realists or naturalists.

2

The Evolution of Modernism

Part of the newness of late nineteenth-century fiction stemmed from what appeared to be new subject matter. Real—and often common—characters were becoming important: the frustrated New England farm wife, the mining camp desperado, the struggling businessman. Women, working men, blacks, Native Americans, immigrants—nontraditional characters appeared in this fiction because they gave writers a means of working with new concerns. Economics—the all-too-appreciable differences between the great wealth of the capitalists and the unremitting poverty of laborers and farmers—struck writers as essential subject matter, as did that of the New Woman. Because women now had the choice of being educated and/or professional, men and women readers alike were fascinated by women characters who might be as self-directed as men. The economic question and the woman question were new and central sources of subjects.[1]

Another traditional theme—the relationship between character and nature—had been changed through urbanization. The great population shift to the city, and the impersonality of that location, gave writers different ideas about the value of place. Theodore Dreiser's *Sister Carrie* (1900) seemed to blame urban life in part for the loss of Carrie's personal values. In early twentieth-century literature, Chicago, and later New York, stood for evil or at least the possibility of evil. In contrast, ownership of land became more desirable.

Stephen Crane's *Red Badge of Courage* signaled another topic for the innovative writer. In Crane's handling of the war theme, he chose not the broad canvas that might include some acts of heroism but rather the single character whose behavior illustrated only his motivation by fear. Crane had earlier written about the effects of urbanization on fragile human beings in *Maggie, A Girl of the Streets,* and he continued to pit characters against forces that were inexplicable, as well as uncontrollable (as in "The Open Boat" and "The

Blue Hotel"). Crane's fatalism, drawn with stark lines and in nonliterary language, was his contribution to the new literature; his terse, emphatic poems may have been more influential than his fiction.

Frank Norris and Jack London also stressed the irresistible forces that preyed on the human being, setting their characters in contexts that almost prevented the use of free will. Norris in *Moran of the Lady Letty* (1898) and *McTeague* (1899) stressed naturalistic beliefs, but in *The Octopus* (1901) and *The Pit* (1903) he examined human drives for economic motives and drew ideas from sociology. Hamlin Garland's almost unrelieved naturalism, which he called veritism, was illustrated best in the characters of his *Main-Travelled Roads* (1891), people whose lives are frustrated by poverty or hostile nature.

The impetus for modernism came less from these texts, however—except in their unrelieved tone of disaster—than from realistic fiction, that written by William Dean Howells, Henry Adams (particularly his memoirs), Henry James, and the important and best-selling "progressive" women writers: Edith Wharton, Sarah Orne Jewett, Mary E. Wilkins Freeman, Kate Chopin, and Ellen Glasgow. Their interest in a character's psychological motivation led to a different concept of the role of narrator. The storyteller became an observer rather than a presence that guided the reader's interpretation, and style seemed to be reportorial—to avoid the sense that the narrator was influencing the reader's perceptions. If the psychological delineation meant that the character was to be seen as the victim or at least the product of external forces, the writer had some responsibility to include social commentary as part of text.

With Howells, the theme of living within the city and being successful attracted readers, but his sometimes tedious detail antagonized the modernist, who praised selection over repetition. Henry Adams's treatment of the clear conflicts between technocracy and humanism—imaged so effectively in the Virgin and the dynamo—became a touchstone for modernist thinking, but his memoirs also attracted modern readers because he chose to speak about his own ambivalence about the world of the twentieth century. Adams's candor, as both character and author, amazed many of his readers, as did his criticism of the view of history as evolutionary (in both *Mont-Saint-Michel and Chartres* in 1904 and in *The*

Education of Henry Adams, published privately in 1907 and publicly in 1918).

Henry James was the most important of these three writers because he appreciated how essential the portrayal of nuance (as separate from detail) was to character. Modern readers respected the lengths to which James would go to present definitive characterization. James's characters opened to the reader as if they were living people. His narrators did not explain personalities, or at least they did not simply explain personalities, but the reader had the opportunity to see the characters in so many situations that he or she was able to predict their choices and actions. Choosing apparently slight scenes, James worked with conviction and authority through plots that consisted of various life choices. And because so many of his characters were slight, with little intrinsic interest, modernists learned what kinds of characters could be used in fiction that depended for its effect on suggestion, on the presentation of the epiphanic moment. They learned that a restrained narrative, properly handled, could become luminous.

Part of James's effectiveness as writer stemmed from his belief that human consciousness developed in nonlinear patterns. What a character knew depended not on how many years he or she had lived but on how many moments of being, how many epiphanies, had been experienced.[2] These moments of recognition might take pages to describe, but the resolution of many of James's characters' dilemmas, as well as their lives, occurred on the basis of these ephemeral turnings. For James, as for the modernists, circularity, layers of metaphor, and repetition and nuance were more common narrative devices than were linear plot lines.[3]

The power of James's fiction rested partly on the reader's ability to understand character from oblique signs, almost in a kind of shorthand. His fiction often operated through irony, much of it dramatic irony. James's characters seemed not to comprehend what was happening to them; because they did not know enough, they could not see enough of any pattern. The reader, however—a love of sleuthing encouraged by James's fragmentary development of narrative—saw that some information was withheld and that other information appeared unexpectedly. "Reading" James's fiction thus became an intriguing subjective act. The notion of fiction as labyrinth that Jorge Luis Borges was to express much later underlay James's work. And by setting the American consciousness against the European, as he did in *The American, Daisy Miller, Portrait of a Lady,* and much of his last and greatest fiction, James made his American readers see that naiveté and innocence, which he saw as integral to the new American vision, were positive.

James's influence on modernism was greater than that of either Crane or Emily Dickinson (writers whose mastery of the art of concise suggestion was of great import) because he consistently dealt with the most complex of subjects: how to live well and with honor in a world that was barely comprehensible and ultimately without much virtue. It was to become the modernists' primary theme. Characters like Isabel Archer and Lambert Strether were doomed by their own free choice, and yet James's fiction admitted that choice was never free but rather influenced by machinations of the old order—both European and traditional American. In James's fiction, sexual betrayal often imaged the larger betrayal of honor.

James's critical writings also spoke for a flexibility that modernist writers respected and echoed. James believed that whatever convinced the reader was an effective method, that organic form—shape and voice suitable to story or effect—was the desired organization for any writing, and that one approach to writing was through the writer's emotional understanding because any genuine interest the reader felt for a character would be on the basis of shared emotional experience. Modernism was to draw heavily from all these tenets. Ezra Pound showed his respect for James's work by editing a special Henry James number of the *Little Review* in 1918, and in his own essay there, he stated that James had never written an unnecessary word. (Because one of the principles of modernist writing was concision, Pound's praise was even more effulgent.)

In tandem with the influence of Henry James comes that of the best-selling and highly crafted work of women writers Sarah Orne Jewett and Mary E. Wilkins Freeman. Freeman had published forty volumes of work by the time of her death in 1930, and in 1926 she had won the William Dean Howells Gold Medal for Fiction. Jewett and Freeman concentrated on the intricacies of women's lives—real and common lives—often lived in isolation or at least within modest family circles, and their fiction lacked the romance of more sensational characters or plots. Readers, however, did not mind.[4]

They admired the skill and the realism with which the stories were told, and they were drawn to these characters whose lives mirrored their own. Sharing with James an interest in psychological motivation, women writers tended to be even more oblique. Less was stated, partly because women writers consistently disguise personal knowledge (the "anxiety of authorship" Gilbert and Gubar described nearly a century later[5]), and meaning was often caught in a symbol or an image. Like James's golden bowl, Jewett's white heron was an expansive and open image—here, one that caught the conflict between sexuality and duty in women's lives. Her *The Country of the Pointed Firs* (1896) became the prototype for the linked story group that can also be considered a novel (Sherwood Anderson's *Winesburg, Ohio;* Hemingway's *In Our Time;* Jean Toomer's *Cane*).

The revival of the women's movement in the 1890s led to great interest in fiction about women characters. In addition to the strong market, an unusual camaraderie among Jewett, Freeman, and Annie Fields and younger writers such as Willa Cather, Susan Glaspell, and Edith Wharton set up a network that encouraged women to write. The prosperity of magazine fiction, which provided an almost limitless market for stories about women, helped these writers and others to support themselves. Charlotte Perkins Gilman, the grand-niece of Harriet Beecher Stowe, combined her writing of fiction with her professional work as an economist and in addition to her moving "The Yellow Wallpaper" wrote *Women and Economics* (1898), *Concerning Children* (1900), *The Home: Its Work and Influence* (1903), and *Human Work* (1904). Women's fiction dealt with the major social question of the turn of the century: the position of women, which encompassed such issues as the appropriate age for a woman to marry, the number of children to have, the use to be gained from greater life expectancy, and the basic fact that women's working had become respectable.

Although women readers appeared ready for almost any theme in fiction, Kate Chopin's 1899 *The Awakening* found those readers' limits. When Edna Pontellier chose death by drowning rather than life with her husband and children, or with a lover, Chopin's readers were incensed. They did not approve the sexual and emotional freedom Edna demanded for herself, and their censure effectively ended Chopin's career as writer. (After the furor over *The Awakening*, Chopin wrote very litte, and lived only a few years longer.)

For the most part, women's fiction was enthusiastically received, provided it appeared to maintain the age-old formulas of romance. The desirable ending of a woman's life, and of a novel, was marriage. If the woman protagonist would not, or could not, marry, she probably died—but that death should be unhappy, not freely chosen, as was Edna's. Women writers learned from the reaction to Chopin's novel and wrote the expected fictions for another twenty years, but they did so increasingly with tongue in cheek. Their employment of irony allowed them to write one kind of fiction under the guise of another. Edith Wharton's *The House of Mirth* (1905) is a good example of the kind of novel her readers would accept (would, in fact, make into a best-seller) while the fiction was also satisfying a more critical readership.

Some readers found in Wharton's Lily Bart the epitome of the unwise virgin, the woman whose role in society was to marry well but whose sense of self and independence kept her from doing so. Lawrence Selden (the "antihero," in Wharton's phrase) could easily have married Lily at several places in the novel, and thereby have "saved" her, but he had no will to propose. Although Wharton shows clearly that Selden is an ineffectual man, a talker who never acts, he still appears to be a good man, if only because he nominally believed in a woman's right to choose her own life. Compared with the other male characters in *The House of Mirth*, Selden is less objectionable, but he is hardly positive. Wharton makes the implicit charge that Selden has allowed Lily to die by adding the brilliant final chapter, which seems to focus on Selden's sorrow as he views Lily's dead body. The length of that final chapter only, in fact, emphasizes Lily's death. Selden may be sorry, but Lily is dead—needlessly.

In this early novel Wharton achieved the apex of effective irony. It is entirely possible for readers to see *The House of Mirth* as traditional romance, with the foolish woman losing everything because she does not follow society's dictates and marry an appropriate man. But it is also possible to read the text as ironic, with nothing but condemnation for those who do succeed within the hypocritical culture, Selden included. In that context, Lily's death becomes a severe indictment of both her culture and her would-be lover.

Wharton was such an expert writer that she could walk the line between traditional and ironic fiction without readers' realizing where her personal sentiments lay. She drew from other women writers and their craft—those contemporary with her, as well as Jane Austen and George Eliot—and created fiction that was strikingly ironic and difficult so far as its techniques were concerned. In her narrator's supposed objectivity and her frequent use of open-ended scenes, Wharton allowed readers to create meaning for her text. In keeping her characterization external, avoiding the use of James's stream-of-consciousness method (which would have made her side too obviously with her women characters), she was able to pretend that characters could be viewed in more than one way.

Ellen Glasgow, who published her first novel in 1897 and then wrote a new book every two or three years until the 1940s, also used heavy irony. Said to represent the southern school of realism, Glasgow evolved a mixture of ironic and conventional presentational strategies that, as Wharton's techniques did, allowed her to keep a conservative readership while yet attracting many new, modern readers. Her 1913 *Virginia,* that lament for the traditional position of a wife; the 1925 *Barren Ground,* which insists that women can live profitable lives without marriage; and her 1932 *The Sheltered Life,* which gives betrayed women the right to kill their cheating husbands, were important texts for other women readers and writers.

Both Glasgow and Wharton used the device of writing as if a male character were the protagonist of, particularly, their early novels. That seldom was the case (often reader interest was divided between a male character and a female), but because "serious" fiction usually dealt with male characters and because both Wharton and Glasgow wanted to be considered serious novelists, they felt compelled to write about male characters to a certain extent. In the balancing of scene and of narrative act, they often create unexpected emphases and situations so that readers must concentrate on the implicatons of relationships and events.[6] Because Wharton and Glasgow were always among the best-selling novelists of any given year, the impact of their novels on younger writers was important. F. Scott Fitzgerald, for one, listed Wharton and Willa Cather in the highest category of his "genius" list, in a position equaled only by Hemingway, Mencken, Ford Madox Ford, and Thomas A. Edison.[7]

The similarities between Wharton and Cather are striking. Cather had written for magazines and newspapers, besides teaching English in Pittsburgh high schools, and between 1909 and 1912 was on the editorial board at *McClure's Magazine.* She was nearly forty when she resigned from that post to write fiction and knew well work by other women writers. When she published *O Pioneers!* in 1913, it looked as if she were drawing on her adolescence, which she spent in Nebraska, and on her interest in the immigrant experience. But Cather's treatment of Alexandra Bergson, a Norwegian immigrant, and that of Thea Kronberg in *The Song of the Lark* (1915) were similar not because these were "western" characters, but because they were women protagonists, whose lives were both undramatic and unconventional. Cather's real theme was the conflict inherent in the choices women were forced to make.

Cather's *My Ántonia* made her craft, and her ability to disguise what her story implied, even clearer. Using the obtuse and romantic Jim Burden as narrator, Cather created a fiction that both revealed and obscured its protagonist. If a reader were to rely on Jim's recounting, he or she would never understand the power and sacrifice of Ántonia's life because Burden himself does not understand the story. (His self-satisfied postscript to her story, in which he and her husband and children become friends, leaves Ántonia out entirely, beyond picturing her as some earth mother in residence.) Cather's experimentation with point of view—the remarkable device of having the Widow Steavens provide the most wrenching story, of Ántonia's betrayal—marks this as a classic modernist text.

F. Scott Fitzgerald learned a great deal from *My Ántonia*—and from Cather's *A Lost Lady*, in which the story is again told through the eyes of a male character rather than from the perspective of the woman protagonist—when he created Nick Carraway to narrate *The Great Gatsby*. The double novel, the story of two characters inextricably interwoven, was a useful form, but in the case of Cather's using it to allow a male character to tell a woman's story, it was probably misleading. Her structure allowed her narrative to remain socially conservative (the male narrator's views represented mainstream opinion, judging and lamenting the woman's choices). Cather as author was then able to cast doubt on the premise that a male narrator could tell a woman's story accurately.

For instance, Jim sees the country roads—along which migrants, including Ántonia, labor unendingly—as "roads to freedom," bordered with sunflowers. The reader knows that Jim has never worked in that countryside. The child of a middle-class family, destined to be educated and sent away from the prairie, he has shared none of the immigrant families' experiences. Ironically, during their childhood, Ántonia was the storyteller, not Jim. As he recalled, "We all liked Tony's stories. her voice had a peculiarly engaging quality; it was deep, a little husky, and one always heard the breath vibrating behind it. Everything she said seemed to come right out of her heart."[8] The stories Ántonia tells are so realistic as to be macabre. They are about the grotesques of the farm life, far from the happy-ending placebos that Jim chooses to recount. The discrepancy between what Ántonia tells when they are growing up, and what Jim fashions in his maturity, warns the reader that the latter's accounts are not trustworthy. Nostalgia has colored his memories.

In both *My Ántonia* and *A Lost Lady*, the narrator is not only male; he is a young male who, supposedly, matures as the story develops. First, the romantic adolescent is responsible for the narration; then the adult male whose life has been reasonably pleasant. Each tells the account of a complex woman. The result of this narrative control is that the reader mistrusts all information that comes by way of this narrator. The novel becomes a fragmented assortment of pieces of text, and the reader's work is to put those pieces together reasonably. For all its smooth delivery of event, both of Cather's novels are as intricately structured as any modernist fiction.

Cather's language is also misleadingly effortless in its polish and choice of diction. Because the narrators are educated boys and men, living with well-educated families and heading themselves for polite social lives, their word choice is appropriate. Occasionally the reader hears the real words of Ántonia and Marian Forrester, but those episodes serve only to point up the differences between the women as they are "recollected" by the narrators and the characters as they existed in their own language and being. For instance, when Marian comes to the law office to use the telephone after Frank Ellinger has married, Niel would have used different language and a different set of circumstances to remember that episode. As it is, he cuts the telephone lines with scissors before Marian can tell Frank off completely—saying he does not want the telephone operator to know the story. Her emphatic dialogue leaves no question as to her anger that her lover has married ("Play safe! When have you ever played anything else? You know, Frank, the truth is that you're a coward; a great, hulking coward. Do you hear me? I want you to hear"). In response to this powerful scene,

Niel says only, "For once he had been quick enough; he had saved her."[9] Cutting telephone lines does not save the angry woman at all, and her collapse shows the agony of rage she suffers. The emotional lives of both Ántonia and Marian are so far removed from the understanding of their narrators that Cather barely escapes being cynical. As *My Ántonia* ends, for example, Jim Burden is filled with self-congratulatory good feeling: he has returned, and he has befriended Ántonia and her family and her husband, Cuzak. He thinks with pleasure on the rest of his life in that role of friend: "My mind was full of pleasant things; trips I meant to take with the Cuzak boys, in the Bad Lands and up on the Stinking Water. There were enough Cuzaks to play with for a long while yet. Even after the boys grew up, there would always be Cuzak himself!" (370). The irony of Jim's coming to find Ántonia and ending up with a ready-made family of young boys who adore him, or another male comrade he can feel superior to, points again to the unsettling kind of characterization Cather allows in the text. Ántonia was never anything other than a male appendage— someone's daughter, someone's sister, someone's servant girl, someone's mother and wife. In the highest praise Jim is possible of giving, he says to her, "I think of you more often than anyone else in this part of the world. I'd have liked to have you for a sweetheart, or a wife, or my mother or my sister—*anything that a woman can be to a man*" (321; emphasis added).

Cather's power rests in her sly subversion of the family romance, the ideal of women dependent on men—stories and lives told by the men in them—even while she managed to create women as tough and enduring as any characters in modern novels. The real women characters in Cather's novels contrast brilliantly with the men who tell their stories, or at least parts of their stories, but we sense the contrast only in the unwritten and untold segments of the tales. Even with titles that seemingly point to these women characters, Cather's novels are usually ironic tapestries of the lives of men, seeing their successes and failures in the terms of the life of some woman who played a unique role in their development.

In her critical essays collected in *Not Under Forty*, Cather makes clear that she learned to write from figures other than the realists. "Every writer who is an artist knows that his 'power of observation' and his 'power of description' form but a low part of his equipment," she notes in one section. "If the novel is a form of imaginative art, it cannot be at the same time a vivid and brilliant form of journalism. Out of the teeming, gleaming stream of the present it must select the eternal material of art."[10]

One has the sense that Cather is selecting scenes and episodes consciously; very little is left up to chance. It is important, for instance, for the reader to know about the sexual episodes in Ántonia's story because she is faced with them, and she has no qualms about putting such events into language. That the reader learns about the macabre deaths of the Cutters near the close of *My Ántonia* provides another gloss on marriage, on the controlling power of a husband, as Ántonia had experienced it in her own life. Cather implies that Jim would not have been able to tell the story, even if he had known it.

The same sense of high selection lies at the heart of the powerful effect of Gertrude Stein's *Three Lives*. Written early in the decade, though not published until 1909, her montage of three separate women's stories immediately attracted other writers. Stein was motivated by a fascination with, and knowledge of, psychology and the work in that field she had done as a student of William James at Radcliffe. Here she tried to capture the characters of personae who were far removed from her own psyche. In the fragmented portraits of three lower-class women (two German hired girls and a black from the city), Stein created accuracy through unusual understatement. The good Anna and the gentle Lena lived thoroughly inarticulate lives; they could not have explained what happened to them or what was happening to them even if Stein had given them roles as narrators. Her seemingly distant perspective and her insistent repetition of simple (and often ambiguous) words drew in the reader, forced the reader to create the story. Operating like poetry, Stein's word portraits relentlessly presented. Anna was "good." That was her flaw. Stein's repetition of that adjective throughout her story showed her ironic, even malicious, reversal of traits that society, and the German woman herself, would have seen as positive: hard working, diligent, self-effacing. Stein's culminating irony occurs as the reader watches Anna once she has become a property owner—no longer working for anyone—relinquish her power in that role and die as a result. (She charges so little for the room and board she sells that she literally starves herself in order to make ends meet.)

From the start of her story, "The good Anna . . . led an arduous and troubled life." Although the facts may not explain this (after all, Anna is in charge, with power to do whatever she chooses), Stein's repetition convinces us that the tendency to martyrdom is Anna's bottom nature: "This one little house was always very full with Miss Mathilda, an under servant, stray dogs and cats and Anna's voice that scolded, managed, grumbled all day long." "Anna Federner, this good Anna, was of solid lower middle-class south german stock." Soon, however, she is described as having a "worn, thin, lined, determined face," and by the end of her story, the word *good* is used infrequently, and she has an "irritable, strained, worn-out body" as she dies.[11]

Description in "The Gentle Lena" opens the story: "Lena was patient, gentle, sweet and german" (239). The indiscriminate order suggests a pattern of unpredictability that continues throughout the story until Lena dies. Unmissed and unmourned, the gentle woman marks Stein's harshest censure for the patriarchal German culture, one that cares only that its children are healthy and does not mourn for their mother. Stein was right in placing "The Gentle Lena" last—though it was written second—because its impact is devastating.

"Melanctha," the longest story and the center of the text, is also effective for its style and its presentation of the relationship between Jeff Campbell, a doctor, and Melanctha Herbert. The story reads with a definite vernacular rhythm, and the speech patterns of Jeff and Melanctha are easily distinguished. (Jeff is the worrier, the abstract thinker, who tries to find reassurance by going over and over his dialogue with Melanctha. She is the actor, a forerunner for Faulkner's Addie Bundren, both women united in their mistrust of words. Melanctha insists that she is what she is, and that if Jeff cannot accept that knowledge, their relationship is over). On the issue of Stein's having created accurate black speech, Claude Mc-Kay said in his 1937 memoir that Jeff and Melanctha might just as well have been Jewish for all the traits of black speech he could find:

"When I came to examine "Melanctha" . . . I could not see wherein it was what it was cracked up to be. In "Melanctha" Gertrude Stein reproduced a number of the common phrases relating to Negroes, such as: "boundless joy of Negroes," "unmorality of black people," "black childish," "big black virile," "joyous Negro," "black and evil," "black heat," "abandoned laughter," "Negro sunshine," all prettily framed in a tricked-out style. . . . The mulatto, Jeff Campbell—he is not typical of mulattoes I have known anywhere. He reminds me more of a type of white lover described by colored women.[12]

Stein achieved seemingly intimate portraits of women and their lives through exacting and surprising language, relying entirely on the verbal representation rather than the scenic. Her insistent language drives home the adjectives and nouns she wants us to have for each character. Though among her earliest work, *Three Lives* also introduces irony because each of these stories ends in deaths that are in no way surprising, deaths we have been building toward from the first of each work. The author's ability to locate, and describe, the roots that led to death and disaffiliation marked her as an important modernist writer, well before modernism existed.

Sherwood Anderson first found Stein's poems when his brother sent him her 1914 collection, *Tender Buttons*, and while he was amazed at the effects single words had in those poetic descriptions, he borrowed more for his own writing from her *Three Lives*. The common and undistinguished characters, made vivid through apt word choice and rhythms germane to their lives, appeared frequently in Anderson's seminal modernist text, *Winesburg, Ohio*, in 1919. What Anderson recreated in that text was Stein's reliance on mood, figures of speech, and refrain lines: "Snow lay deep in the streets of Winesburg. It had begun to snow about ten o'clock in the morning and a wind sprang up and blew the snow in clouds along Main Street. . . . 'Snow will bring the people into town on Saturday. . . . Snow will be good for the wheat.' "[13]

In "The Teacher" Anderson creates a snow-bound isolation to image the isolation of George Willard and Kate Swift, the teacher of the title. All the action occurs on a snowy night; all the emotions are bleak, and remain so: contact between the two characters is never made. The central image—for the emotions of the people as well as for the setting—occurs early: "By nine o'clock of that evening snow lay deep in the streets and the weather had become bitter cold. It was difficult to walk about. The stores were dark and the people crawled away to their houses" (186). Another technique Anderson uses well, reminiscent of Stein, is the combination of descriptive tag with the revealing central image: "Wing Biddlebaum talked much with his hands. The slender expressive fingers, forever active, forever striving to conceal themselves in his pockets or behind his back, came forth and became the piston rods of his machinery of expression" (9). Seldom does Anderson do this better, combining the graphic image with the figurative. This passage follows another good simile—"With a kind of wriggle, like a fish returned to the brook by a fisherman, Biddlebaum the silent began to talk"—and allows Anderson the choice of a succinct and emphatic introduction: "The story of Wing Biddlebaum is a story of hands" (9).

Unlike Stein, Anderson often uses images to create both mood and character, avoiding the repeated detail that becomes a refrain: Wing's hands, Enoch Robinson's room, Reverend Hartman's window, Kate Swift's anger, Elizabeth Willard's makeup. By presenting the key to each life graphically instead of rhetorically, Anderson creates a sharp impact and swift pace. The method provides an inherent condensation.

When Anderson does use refrain, it is likely to be within dialogue. Elizabeth Willard's inarticulate gropings to reach her son contrast painfully with the commitment of her plot to kill her husband with a scissors, if she must, to free her son. All she manages to say is "I think you had better go out among the boys. You are too much indoors" (184). Similarly, all Melanctha ever says is, "All I can do now, Jeff, is to keep certainly with my believing you are good always, Jeff" (160). Unfortunately, Jeff has many more pages of convoluted rhetoric as he attempts to understand. Stein's reason for her interest in such dialogue fits logically with her attempt to present the precise attitude of each character, at each moment in question:

I began to get enormously interested in hearing how everybody said the same thing over and over again with infinite variations but over and over again until finally if you listened with great intensity you could hear it rise and fall and tell all that there was inside them, not so much by the actual words they said or the thoughts they had but by the movement of their thoughts and words endlessly the same and endlessly different.[14]

Repeatedly in Anderson's *Winesburg* stories, when the characters are in a position to reach each other, language fails them. Unrelieved, they turn away, all of them, even George Willard as he says his farewells to Helen White in "Sophistication":

> The boy's voice failed and in silence the two came back into town and went along the street to Helen White's house. At the gate he tried to say something impressive. Speeches he had thought out came into his head, but they seemed utterly pointless. "I thought—I used to think—I had it in my mind you would marry Seth Richmond. Now I know you won't" was all he could find to say as she went through the gate and toward the door of her house. (290)

It is this mood of isolation, of emotional poverty, that haunts the stories of *Winesburg* and gives them their strongest bond with Stein's *Three Lives*. When Anderson wrote that his interest in fiction was never in plot but rather in "human nature, the strange little whims, tragedies and comedies of life itself," he was casting his lot with Stein's good Anna, Melanctha, and especially with the gentle Lena.[15]

Stein's understated presentation of the inarticulate Lena's death caps her skill in shaping style to mood. "There were really bad days for poor Lena" (275), she states cryptically; "Lena always was more and more lifeless and Herman now mostly never thought about her" (278). The death of the marriage precedes Lena's physical death, and Stein's stolid monosyllabics perfectly reflect the dulling apathy: "When it was all over Lena had died, too, and nobody knew just how it had happened to her" (279).

Life as something "happening to" characters sets the mood as well for Anderson's equally exhausted protagonist in "Death in the Woods." One of his strongest stories, this account of old woman Grimes resembles Stein's Lena in that Mrs. Grimes was also a bound girl, victimized in a German farmer's house, accepting marriage as the lesser of the all too prevalent evils. But the reality of her marriage, and her life, became so oppressive that her death by freezing was simple relief.

Anderson's techniques in "Death in the Woods" are particularly Stein-like. His opening is marked by the sentence subject repetition that Stein used so effectively, with the added irony that all of the subjects are the word *she* rather than Mrs. Grimes's given name. So nondescript is the character that he does not name her:

> She was an old woman and lived on a farm near the town in which I lived. All country and small-town people have such old women, but no one knows much about them. Such an old woman comes into town driving an old worn-out horse or she comes afoot carrying a basket. She may own a few hens and have eggs to sell. She brings them in a basket and takes them to a grocer. There she trades them in. She gets some salt pork and some beans. Then she gets a pound or two of sugar and some flour.[16]

The poignancy of the woman's nameless position in her culture is signaled further by Anderson's comment, "No one gave her a lift. People drive right down a road and never notice an old woman like that" (533).

Anderson's key device in his presentation of the old woman is his refrain: "Then she settled down to feed stock. That was her job. . . . Every moment of every day, as a young girl, was spent feeding something" (533). Bleak as this image of continuous labor is, the tone darkens when Anderson adds to it the threat of her husband's violence when she fails to keep things fed, and the threat in her sexual relationship with him.

Had Anderson ended the story in the early years of the marriage, the similarities with Stein's Lena would be even more striking. But the story goes on, unrelieved, to prove repeatedly that the Grimes wife has exchanged her life of labor for one of absurd abysmal struggle, to keep things alive even when her own life has become meaningless:

Well, things had to be fed. Men had to be fed, and the horses that weren't any good but maybe could be traded off, and the poor thin cow that hadn't given any milk for three months.
Horses, cows, pigs, dogs, men (534).

In later sections of the story, Anderson juxtaposes the old woman's treatment at the hands of her family with her treatment by the apparently savage farm dogs. Brutalized as she has been by both her husband and her son, the old woman was yet saved from the violence that might have been expected from the pack of dogs by the animals themselves. "The dogs had not touched her body,"

Anderson reports with a Stein-like bluntness (542). His use of sentence variation to create the rhythms of the running dogs and his use of parallel sentence structure also suggest that he is writing with more care than he sometimes did.

In Anderson's work, and in much of that written by other later modernists, Stein's influence seems clear. That ability to repeat without being quite repetitious, that trick of catching character in a phrase or idiom, that rare gift of writing intentionally as if there were no intention: Stein excelled in all these. She was all intention; every effect was contrived. Hemingway and Faulkner and Anderson were to learn from her that calculation helped create the totality of impact that was the aim of modern writing. Whether that total impact was known as organic form or experimental structure, it owed at least some thanks to Stein, who insisted that meaning in any text accrued in part not from what was said but from the way language gave that meaning expression.

3

From Poetry to Prose

Another of the origins of modern fiction was poetry written early in the twentieth century. The revolution in poetry occurred more than a decade before that in prose. As John Dos Passos reminisced in his memoirs, "Poetry was more important than submarines or war guilt or brave little Belgium or the big board on the New York stock exchange."[1] In the poetic revolution, post-Victorian formalism gave way to free verse; didactic moralizing disappeared before a sharply crystallized image; and poems came to be about the common people and events of daily life instead of highly refined literary subjects like love, death, and nature.

By 1913, the varieties of this free-form poetry—whether championed by T. E. Hulme, F. S. Flint, and Ford Madox Ford, or the American contingent of Ezra Pound, H.D., T. S. Eliot, Carl Sandburg, Robert Frost, Amy Lowell, or William Carlos Williams—became known as imagism. In fact, in 1913, the year America was shaken by the Armory Show and the first English translation of Freud's *Interpretation of Dreams, Poetry* magazine published the imagist manifesto, ascribed then to both F. S. Flint and Pound.

Pound's important essay in *Poetry* defined the image as "that which presents an intellectual and emotional complex in an instant of time." He continued, "The point of Imagisme is that it does not use images *as ornaments*. The image is itself the speech." By stressing the immediacy of the image, Pound insisted that art built from such depictions was never to be static; it should instead embody the speed consistent with a moving eye or a moving mind: "It is the presentation of such a 'complex' instantaneously which gives the sense of sudden liberation; that sense of freedom from time limits and space limits; that sense of *sudden growth*, which we experience in the presence of the greatest works of art."[2]

In the accompanying essay, which was ascribed to Flint, the three "rules" of imagism appeared:

1. Direct treatment of the "thing," whether subjective or objective.
2. To use absolutely no word that does not contribute to the presentation.
3. As regarding rhythm: to compose in the sequence of the musical phrase, not in sequence of a metronome.[3]

Flint explained that the second point was primary, giving as example the fact that an imagist poet could often rewrite ordinary verse "using about ten words to another poet's fifty." The principle of *vers libre*, which attracted much critical attention, was one way to attain organic form, a shape consistent with the mood and subject being expressed in the poem.

Aside from freeing poetry from prescribed rhyme and rhythm patterns that were sometimes unnatural to the phrasing of American English, imagism was important for its emphasis on concentration, on the necessity for the poet to know his or her craft, and on the use of the natural, spoken idiom. Most of Pound's essay relates to ways of cutting words, of making every word in a poem work. "Go in fear of abstractions," he warns. "Use either no ornament or good ornament"; "Don't be descriptive"; "Present."[4] The poet became a polisher of gems, as did the prose writer. Hemingway's vignettes and stories in *In Our Time* (1925) are good examples.

Literary history provides several reasons for sensing a firm relationship between the theory of imagism and prose styles of a decade later. No comparable body of prose theory existed so early. Percy Lubbock's *The Craft of Fiction* was not published until 1921; E. M. Forster's *Aspects of the Novel*, in 1927; and Henry James's prefaces were not well known in America, despite the fact that Pound had edited a special James issue of the *Little Review* in 1917–18. Writers were reading *Poetry*, the *Criterion*, the *Dial*, the *Little Review*, the *Double Dealer*, *Reedy's Mirror*, and other little magazines whose prose usually concerned innovation in poetry. Eliot, Pound, and Ford Madox Ford themselves wrote hundreds of critical pieces between 1910 and 1930. As Jay McCormick, writing in *The Middle Distance*, concludes, "The unquestioned veracity and propriety of poetic experiment" combined with all the poetic theory available "conspired to urge" many prose writers to experiment.[5]

Another quality of the writing of the 1920s that may be a corollary to this point is that writers then attempted to write everything. They were comparatively unself-conscious of the differences among genres: Eliot's move into essay and drama; Williams's attempts at novels, short stories, history, essay, drama, biography; H.D.'s increasing fascination with fiction and film criticism; cummings's novel and plays; D. H. Lawrence, Joyce, and Stein as ready to try poetry as fiction. Because so many writers worked in more than one genre, they were interested in developments everywhere, and the transfer of principles and devices from one mode to another was much easier than it might have been in a period more conscious of the boundaries of genre.

Many important modernist novelists also began their writing careers as poets. Hemingway's first book was *Three Stories & Ten Poems* (1923), and he at least claimed to write poetry throughout his life. Faulkner wrote only poetry for over a decade, encouraged early by the *New Republic*'s acceptance of a poem. He often referred to himself as a poet, or a "failed poet"; and his papers contain drafts of numerous unpublished and unfinished poems. His first book was the 1924 poem sequence, *A Marble Faun*, and critic Judith Sensibar has proven recently how integral to his fiction-writing process was his crafting of long poem sequences.[6] In 1917, John Dos Passos made his first appearance in print as one of the *Eight Harvard Poets*; and his own early poem collection, *A Pushcart at the Curb* (1922), includes a wide range of free-form poems, many grouped together in sequences that have a narrative strategy, others foreshadowing the Whitmanic rhythms of the prose-poem biographies of *U.S.A.*

There is also ample proof that each of these three novelists was a staunch admirer of Ezra Pound, Pound being perhaps the only one of Hemingway's early literary mentors whom he never turned against. Joseph Blotner records that Faulkner followed Pound through the streets of Paris, though he never got up enough courage to approach the leader of modern letters. Understanding this allegiance and seeing these novelists in the context of modern poetry may better enable us to appreciate the impact Eliot's *The Waste Land* had on the world of modern writing.[7]

While there is great variation in the poems of Dos Passos and Faulkner, both wrote at least a few classic imagist poems early in their careers. Dos Passos's brief image from "Winter in Castile" illustrates the concrete made poetic, the use of the detailed presentation of an image rather than the use of an abstract theme:

> The weazened old woman without teeth
> who shivers on the windy street corner
> displays her roasted chestnuts invitingly
> like marriageable daughters.[8]

So too does Hemingway's poem "On Wedding Gifts," reminiscent of the work of e. e. cummings in that even punctuation marks are used as words:

> Three traveling clocks
> Tick
> On the mantelpiece
> Comma
> But the young man is starving.[9]

Although many of Faulkner's poems reflect his interest in the romantics, several of his poems, with his essays, show his knowledge and approval of the imagist tenets, as does the almost oriental "XXII" from *A Green Bough:*

> I see your face through the twilight of my mind,
> A dusk of forgotten things, remembered things;
> It is a corridor dark and cool with music
> And too dim for sight,
> That leads me to a door which brings
> You, clothed in quiet sound for my delight.[10]

These key points from the imagist tenets can easily be extended into prose theory: (1) the centrality of the image, a concrete representation as opposed to an abstraction; (2) the objectivity of presentation; (3) juxtaposition as a means of connecting single images, the placing of image against image with no literal transition so that the reader's apprehension of meaning depends on an immediate response to the montage of concrete detail; (4) *organ base,* Pound's notion that every piece of writing has a controlling tone and a shape that reflects its meaning; and (5) simplicity, rooted in directness and in the avoidance of poetic diction and subject matter. Such simplicity is to be nonallusive, yet it is subtle and sophisticated. As Pound explained,

There are various kinds of clarity. There is the clarity of the request: Send me four pounds of ten-penny nails. And there is the syntactical simplicity of the request: Buy me the kind of Rembrandt I like. This last is an utter cryptogram. It presupposes a more complex and intimate understanding of the speaker than most of us ever acquire of anyone. It has as many meanings, almost, as there are persons who might speak it. . . . It is the almost constant labor of the prose artist to translate this latter kind of clarity into the former; to say "Send me the kind of Rembrandt I like" in the terms of "Send me four pounds of ten-penny nails."[11]

It was Pound who early described Hemingway as an "imagist" in his fiction.[12] To show the kinds of extension possible from this poetic doctrine into fiction, let us begin with Hemingway's work.

1. For image, read scene. In modern writing, the sharply etched and definitely located scene, complete with dialogue or monologue, carries whole stories, sometimes entire novels. As William J. Handy points out, "Most modern fiction is better seen as a single image than as a linear progression." Handy compares the fictional scene with the poetic image and points out too how much information can be conveyed through a tightly structured presentation.[13] Hemingway was the obvious master of scene as image: the desolate limestone foundations of the mill at Horton's Bay in "The End of Something" ("There's our old ruin, Nick," Marjorie said, on the way to the end of their relationship); the "clean, well-lighted place" and all its implications for the lonely old men; the burned-out town of Seney, Michigan, that is the starting point of recovery for the burned-out Nick of "Big Two-Hearted River." In each of these stories, geographical scene becomes an image, is an image for the emotional drive of the narrative.[14]

2. Meaning is presented directly. It is not told or interpreted by a didactic narrator. Hemingway's morals are seldom explicit. By resting on the impact of a scene, he avoids commentary. The exhilaration of skiing in "Cross-Country Snow," for example, opens and closes the story, yet this is a story not of freedom but of freedom curtailed. In a few pages of dialogue, Hemingway conveys the tension in the young marriage because of the expected child (the situation so clearly foreshadowed with the appearance of the surly pregnant waitress), and the resulting change in life-style—and in the friendship between Nick and George. The objective correlative is skiing, the epitome of flight in its "rush and sudden swoop" (*In Our Time*, 107).

The danger of presenting the scene, image, or character rather than describing it by a reliable narrator is that a reader may misread or overlook important clues—other images, the progression in their appearance—and find Brett Ashley less than noble, Santiago the victim of foolish pride, or the Indian husband in "Indian Camp" stupid because he kills himself.

3. Juxtaposition, one of the modern artist's most important technical devices, is frequently used in Hemingway's fiction. "Indian Camp" works largely through juxtaposition: whenever the doctor is holding forth with his rational comments, Hemingway opposes a humane, more emotional reaction (from the boy Nick, Uncle George, or the Indian father):

Just then the woman cried out.

"Oh, Daddy, can't you give her something to make her stop screaming?" asked Nick.

"No. I haven't any anaesthetic," his father said. "But her screams are not important. I don't hear them because they are not important."

The husband in the upper bunk rolled over against the wall.[15]

Similarly, in "Soldier's Home," Harold Krebs's reaction to his mother's platitudes is never verbally expressed. It is conveyed only through a graphic one-line description, juxtaposed with the words of her monologue:

"I've worried about you so much, Harold," his mother went on. "I know the temptations you must have been exposed to. I know how weak men are. I know what your own dear grandfather, my own father, told us about the Civil War and I have prayed for you. I pray for you all day long, Harold."

Krebs looked at the bacon fat hardening on his plate. (*In Our Time*, 75)

4. No story or novel can illustrate the concept of *organ base* or organic form, but—from the one-paragraph vignettes of *In Our Time* to the long novels such as *For Whom the Bell Tolls* and *A Farewell to Arms*—Hemingway's fiction surely suggests that the form of each piece of writing grew from the urgencies of its mood and content.

5. The central point about the Hemingway style is based on Pound's notion of simplicity and clarity. Stating complex situations in casual, simple language is the heart of Hemingway's fictional

method and the reason that everyone can "read" Hemingway and still come away with varied explications of what has been read. The emotions presented are seldom simple—but the presentation? Consider this crucial dialogue from "Soldier's Home" in which Krebs and his favorite sister present, in miniature, the story's theme: that people often use love for their personal ends:

> "Am I really your girl?"
> "Sure."
> "Do you love me?"
> "Uh, huh."
> "Will you love me always?"
> "Sure."
> "Will you come over and watch me play indoor?"
> "Maybe."
> "Aw, Hare, you don't love me. If you loved me, you'd want to come over and watch me play indoor." (*In Our Time*, 74)

With Hemingway at his best, the simplest dialogue conveys information, establishes character, presents theme, and creates tempo, even while it appears to be only repeating itself. The author said near the end of his life, "I sometimes think my style is suggestive rather than direct. The reader must often use his imagination or lose the most subtle part of my thought."[16]

Faulkner's fiction serves as a showcase for his belief in organic form. "The stories seem to shape themselves as they go along," he claimed early. "The story will choose its own type of telling, own style. . . . I am convinced that the story invents, compels its own style. Each novel must have 'one single urn or shape.' "[17] Hasn't the confusion that greeted many of Faulkner's novels usually stemmed from the fact that his narrative method was, once again, new? What did Faulkner not try: from the deceptively simple "Grandfather said" that opens *The Reivers* (that last breathless 300-page reminiscence of a single episode in young Lucius Priest's life) to the alternating but basically contrapuntal stories in *The Wild Palms*; the various "blend" novels like *The Unvanquished*, *The Hamlet*, and *Go Down, Moses*; the unwieldy block structure of *A Fable*; the juxtaposition of drama and essay in *Requiem for a Nun*; the multiple-narrator novels *The Town* and *The Mansion*; novels that begin with the denouement, like *Light in August; Pylon,* in which the central observer never has a name; and the variations on the stream-of-consciousness patterns, *The Sound and the Fury, As I Lay Dying,* and *Absalom, Absalom!*

Of all these methods, the last—difficult as it was for readers to follow—was closest to Faulkner's heart, partly because he was one of the few modernists who were able to identify so completely with fictional characters that he could achieve true speech identity. Readers believe Quentin Compson's anguish; they admire Shreve McCannon's restraint; they pity Benjy Compson, as well as Addie Bundren, Darl, and the inarticulate Jewel. But perhaps Faulkner also used the stream-of-consciousness method because it so perfectly presented meaning. As he claimed in a 1931 interview, novelists should "let the characters tell their own stories instead of filling page after page with exposition":

In the future novel, Mr. Faulkner contends, there will be no straight exposition, but instead, objective presentation, by means of soliloquies or speeches of the characters, those of each character printed in a different colored ink. Something of the play technique will thus eliminate much of the author from the story. And the consequent loss of personality? Is not all writing interesting and important only insofar as it expresses the personality of the author? All exclusive of the story, Mr. Faulkner says, is dead weight. What is interesting in Dickens is not the way he takes things, but "those people he wrote about and what they did."[18]

In *The Sound and the Fury,* Faulkner used as key scenes, serving as images, Damuddy's death and funeral, Caddie's coming home from school, Caddie's wedding, father's funeral. "Life"—and not only to the retarded Benjy—is, in Faulkner's presentation, a montage of crucial events; characters find their reality through their reaction to those key scenes. Fragments of conversation, the fragrance of honeysuckle, Caddie's old slipper: the image is, for Faulkner as it is for Hemingway, a primary means of conveying characters' emotions.

With Faulkner, the image is perhaps even more important, partly because his prose rhythm is so steadily ornate, his novels so engagingly long, overpowerful in total. A world of universal meaning is forced into the covers of a single text as Faulkner anguishes over presenting a complete picture—one never even ostensibly simple. What does *Light in August* become without the circles of repetition set against the "straight and simple corridors" of the dangerously oversimplified minds of Doc Hines, Percy Grimm, and Miss Atkins? How much would the novel lose if Hightower had not had his vision, his image of apotheosis, seeing as he finally does the everyman qualities of both Joe Christmas and Percy Grimm? One reason Faulkner's short stories are generally less effective than his novels is that a brief piece of writing cannot contain the whole texture—rhythm, image, and repetition—that is integral to his most successful efforts.

Faulkner tackles the plethora of the modern world's problems, but he also incorporates a raft of nineteenth-century dilemmas as well. His incremental sense of history leads him to build top-heavy structures: where does the present begin? Where has the past left off? How can a person forget his or her history, even if individual choice is to live in the immediate present? Thematically as well as structurally, Faulkner must deal with these issues, which are overwhelming both intellectually and emotionally. Whereas Hemingway pretended that his heroes could exist cut off from their histories and that of their country, assuming a pose against the modern intellectual realization of the interconnectedness of all knowledge and life, Faulkner only absorbed more and more. If the past was only an obsessive vestige of Quentin Compson's consciousness in *The Sound and the Fury*, by the time of *Absalom, Absalom!* it was a torrent of mystery to be unraveled, explicated, understood. Quentin's history became his obsession, with Caddie's life only a slender thread running through it. More dominant threads were those of the southern history itself, the Civil War, the conquest of the land, white patriarchal pride and ownership (of all things, not only land). And by the time of *Go Down, Moses*, Faulkner's need to coalesce all knowledge, all history—black as well as white—brought him to one of his finest achievements.

Approaching the history of the McCaslin family segmentally, Faulkner creates a montage of image/scene, family event, and generational pattern that almost defies interpretation. The fallacy of a person's believing that one can learn from history is etched bitterly throughout this 1942 text because—as in *Absalom, Absalom!*—unreliable narrators and observers are the rule rather than the exception. Faulkner took the modernist aesthetic a step further than any other of his contemporaries: he used objective narrators who were truly objective. They told the ostensible events of the narrative without subjectivity because they never understood the implications of those events. In Faulkner's later novels, all human knowledge is partial.

It might appear that Ike McCaslin knows the full history of the McCaslins because he traces miscegenation and incest through the family ledgers. His knowledge forces him to disclaim his inheritance, in fact, as he relinquishes his rightful property for a dole that barely keeps him and his wife in necessities. Far from being noble, Ike's relinquishment costs him both his marriage and his leadership role among his peers—although Faulkner provides some comfort to his old age by allowing him to play "uncle" to half the county. A man's man, Ike makes the annual hunting party, relearns his important knowledge of the woods, and remembers his life when Sam Fathers was his mentor and guide.

His life is not idyllic, however, and his role is flawed as badly as is that of the other surviving white McCaslin heir, Roth Edmonds. The penultimate section of the novel, "Delta Autumn," depicts Edmonds mirroring the same futile, proud acts of the original McCaslin—denying his child by a mulatto mother (herself an ancestor of the black McCaslin strain), remaining "childless" and purposeless in his haughty and reasonably wealthy domain. His moral code is seriously flawed also when he kills a doe at the end of the hunting scene. Like Ike, Roth has forgotten what it takes to make a man truly complete.

The only other descendant of the McCaslin family is black. Lucas Beauchamp carries the full name of his white ancestor, but were it not for his tough and sensible wife, Molly, he too would go the way of foolish masculine pride. Molly saves him repeatedly—from the sins of avarice, trickery, and pride—and Faulkner uses her frequently to show the modest and long-suffering endurance of which she alone seems capable. Representing the Worsham line, another white family which is more sympathetic to its blacks, Molly draws the tapestry of *Go Down, Moses* to a close with her mourning for her grandson, Samuel, a criminal. In her insistence that he be mourned, that his body be returned and honored in a funeral (and reported in the newspaper), she does the appropriate homage to family, lineage, and kinship. It is telling that any real emotion is shown primarily in this last, title chapter, and in "Pantaloon in Black," the only section not about a McCaslin descendant. There, Rider mourns for his dead wife so deeply that no one else in his culture—black or white—can understand his grieving. His erstwhile suicide is the only answer he finds. Just as in "Go Down, Moses" Gavin Stevens cannot understand the mourning for Samuel, so Rider's all-consuming grief is incomprehensible. Emotion, Faulkner believes, is relentless—and all too rare. And among the McCaslin heirs, it does not exist.

The art that Faulkner uses in *Go Down, Moses* is once again innovative and almost surreal in its effect. In structure and in theme, the novel uses the repetition of lament, the recurring episodes of emotion, and the intractable facade of personalities to stymie the reader. If Faulkner's first question is "What is happening here?" and the second, "Why is it happening?" then the third is "What use will the character's consciousness make of this happening?" Faulkner seems most interested in this last inquiry. Each of his characters is subject to the history of his or her country and time; what each makes of those circumstances determines his or her survival.

Known primarily as the classic imagist poet, H.D.—Hilda Doolittle—wrote a great amount of fiction during the 1920s and the 1930s. Some of it remained unpublished until the 1980s, but her prowess in narrative gradually changed the style and themes of her poetry. From the brief and exact lyrics like "Heat" and "Oread," with deft images crystallizing the meaning of the poem, H.D. moved into the kind of comprehensive webbing of sound and image that characterized "Fragment Thirty-Six," her adaptation of a Sappho poem in translation. In the intricate rhymes that reinforced the sometimes understated content, she wrote poems that were much like her 1920s fiction: "I know not what to do: / to turn and slake / the rage that burns, / with my breath burn / and trouble your cool breath? / so shall I turn and take / snow in my arms? / (is love's gift best?) / yet flake on flake / of snow were comfortless, / did you lie wondering, / wakened yet unawake. / Shall I turn and take / comfortless snow within my arms? / . . . Is love's gift best?"[19]

In *Bid Me to Live, Palimpsest,* and the recently published *HERmione,* the last written in 1927, H.D. brought all her ingenuity with word patterns to play in a seemingly nonlinear text that yet gave her reader everything possible about the character chosen as protagonist. In each, that character is a young, maturing woman, caught in circles of apparent failure (her scientist father and brother see her failure in mathematics as the end for her college career; her mother sees her inept social manner as the end of her success as a desirable woman on the marriage market; her friends see her relationships with men like George [Pound] as unwise). Typical of what Carol Gilligan calls a great difference in the way women perceive their identities—successful in relation to others, not separable or single—Hermione Gart (nicknamed HER) judges her self-worth by her involvement with others.[20] H.D.'s presentation of that involvement is cyclic and interrelated, suggesting in its style the importance of layered connections:

> Her thought, panther-lean cat, strode up ahead of George. Her thought was swifter than George's witty, tricky thought. Thought chased thought like two panthers. Her own thought, swifter than the thought of George, was there beyond him. "You'll never, never catch me." Her faced George with that, standing on the narrowest of woodpaths that twisted (she knew) a narrow trickle of earth-colour across the green and green that was the steady running of swift water, the steady sweeping and seeping and swirling of branches all about her. If George would catch her, then George would be, might yet be something. "It's too hot, Hermione."
>
> Heat seeped up, swept down, swirled about them with the green of branches that was torrid tropic water. Green torrid tropic water where no snow fell, where no hint of cold running streams from high mountains swept down, was swept into and under branches that made curious circle and half circle and whole circle . . . concentric circle of trees above her head. . . . Tree on tree on tree. TREE. I am the Tree of Life. Tree. I am a tree planted by the rivers of water. I am . . . I am . . . HER exactly.[21]

In forcing the reader to follow the circling pattern of Her's thought, H.D. brings a new insistence to reader involvement. More poetic than fictional in her use of language, she chose a tactic far removed from Hemingway's. His choice was subtly to bring readers to understand the power of the image through careful framing. His sentences and paragraphs led the reader to realize the importance of the single detail, the heightened comparison, the surprising metaphor. In H.D.'s work, the reader was asked to recreate the character's thought process and to create necessary emphases from the swirl of seemingly equal words and sentences. It was a technique that privileged its own difficulty, and for H.D. the writing process was never a compromise with any such consideration as reader ability.

In contrast to H.D.'s and Faulkner's often difficult fiction, the work of Dos Passos is relatively easy, even somewhat mechanical. Like Faulkner, Dos Passos is also interested in American history, but history is treated as a somewhat remote and conveniently factual entity. Dos Passos as writer maintains the objectivity the modernists required and chose instead to work out an intricate technical web of conveying that history. In his *U.S.A.* trilogy, he synthesized many of the currents in modern fiction. He used four styles to separate kinds of historical event, and each style was distinctive in appearance and in intention.

Impressionistic stream of consciousness, conveyed without punctuation or capitalization, expresses the "Camera Eye" fragments of what is the writer's autobiography. Tracing, somewhat obscurely, the life of the young man whose birth occurred at the beginning of the new century, these short sections are marked by alliteration, refrainlike repetitions, and the more obvious conventions of poetry:

skating on the pond next the silver company's mills where
there was a funny fuzzy smell from the dump whaleoil soap somebody
said it was used in cleaning the silver knives and spoons and forks
putting shine on them for sale there was shine on the ice early
black ice that rang like a sawblade just scratched white by the
first skaters I couldn't learn to skate and kept falling down
look out for the muckers everybody said Bohunk and Polak
kids put stones in the snowballs write dirty words up on walls do
dirty things up alleys their folks work in the mills
    we clean young American Rover Boys handy with tools
Deerslayers played hockey Boy Scouts and cut figure eights on the
ice Achilles Ajax Agamemnon I couldn't learn to skate and kept
falling down.[22]

Whether Dos Passos is reminiscing about boyhood or manhood, these sections work consistently well. Some of the sharpest writing occurs in the war-related passages, as these opening lines from a later "eye" illustrate:

remembering the gray crooked fingers the thick drip of
blood off the canvas the bubbling when the lungcases try to

breathe the muddy scraps of flesh you put in the ambulance
alive and haul out dead. (*1919*, 118)

More critical comments exist within the "Newsreel" passages
than in the other styles of writing, stressing the irony inherent in
the juxtaposition of elements from songs, news, headlines, over-
heard conversations. Effective as these sections are, the cumulative
ironies are easier to achieve than those within the books considered
as a whole or within the other kinds of sections:

PARIS SHOCKED AT LAST

HARRIMAN SHOWN AS RAIL COLOSSUS

NOTED SWINDLER RUN TO EARTH

TEDDY WIELDS BIG STICK

STRAPHANGERS DEMAND RELIEF

We were sailing along
On moonlight bay
You can hear the voices ringing
They seem to say
You have stolen my heart, now don't go away
Just as we sang
love's
old
sweet
songs
On moonlight bay

MOB LYNCHES AFTER PRAYER
(*42nd Parallel*, 100)

The narrative of the three novels—and there is a clear and substantial plot line—occupies the bulk of the 1,500 pages in the third
style of writing. Here Dos Passos uses a terse direct prose, more
like that of Theodore Dreiser at his simplest than that of either
Hemingway or Faulkner, and identifies each character's story with
his or her name: Mac, Janey, J. Ward Moorhouse, Eleanor Stod-
dard, Charley Anderson, Mary French, and others. As the narratives cross, Dos Passos creates a composite of a diverse national
character.

The fourth style of writing in *U.S.A.* is the prose-poem "biography," usually phrased in Whitmanlike rhythms. Dos Passos chooses as subjects for these sections American heroes such as Frank Lloyd Wright, Thomas A. Edison, Eugene Debs, Randolph Bourne, the Wright brothers, Isadora Duncan, and others whose intellectual or artistic courage led them to discoveries that the modernists admired. This is part of the incantatory ending of the Wright brothers' segment:

> In nineteen-eleven they were back on the dunes
> at Kitty Hawk with a new glider.
> Orville stayed up in the air for nine and a half minutes,
> which remained a long time the record for motorless flight.
> The same year Wilbur died of typhoidfever in Dayton.
> In the rush of new names: Farman, Blériot, Curtiss, Ferber,
> Esnault-Peltrie, Delagrange;
> in the snorting impact of bombs and the whine and rattle
> of shrapnel and the sudden stutter of machineguns after the
> motor's been shut off overhead,
> and we flatten into the mud
> and make ourselves small cowering in the corners of
> ruined walls,
> the Wright brothers passed out of the headlines . . . .
>
> (*Big Money*, 297–98)

Interesting as Dos Passos's various styles were, the openness of his text left many readers bewildered. They could decipher neither relationships among the kinds of writing nor his intention in composing the trilogy as a whole. Misunderstood as much of the best modern fiction was, *U.S.A.* failed for many readers. As T. S. Eliot complained in his preface to Djuna Barnes's controversial novel *Nightwood* in 1939, "A prose that is altogether alive demands something of the reader that the ordinary novel-reader is not prepared to give. . . . This book is so good a novel that only sensibilities trained on poetry can wholly appreciate it."[23]

Unlike Hemingway, Faulkner, H.D., and Dos Passos, Gertrude Stein wrote prose before she turned to poetry. She began writing prose soon after the turn of the century, and her fascination with the sentence, the unit that for her shaped all expression, led her through *Q.E.D.*, *Fernhurst*, *Three Lives*, some portraits, and *The*

Making of Americans. After finishing what she saw as her autobiographical prose, Stein turned to the poetry of *Tender Buttons,* published in 1914. Light years ahead of comparable theorists and
writers, Stein was already impatient at the imagist tenets. William
Carlos Williams was writing about wheelbarrows and crowds at
ballgames, but Stein was describing celery, roast beef, a friend's
umbrella, and space in ways that moved the reader far past the
necessarily concrete and back into the subjective that many modernists were trying to escape: from the tenderness of Stein's affection for Mildred Aldrich, expressed in the language of her lost
umbrella ("A cause and no curve, a cause and loud enough, a
cause and extra a loud clash and an extra wagon, a sign of extra . . . a slender grey and no ribbon")[24] to her often witty descriptions of foods: of roast beef, "In the inside there is sleeping, in the
outside there is reddening, in the morning there is meaning, in
the evening there is feeling. . . . Please be the beef, please beef,
pleasure is not wailing. Please beef, please be carved clear, please
be a case of consideration. . . . A satin sight, what is a trick, no
trick is mountainous and the color, all the rush is in the blood"
(477), or of celery, "Celery tastes tastes where in curled lashes and
little bits and mostly in remains" (491). Many of Stein's poems are
lengthy, sonorous stream-of-consciousness meditations, only indirectly connected with a speaker but grounded entirely in the voice
that appears to be Stein's. Like Faulkner, Stein used rhythms and
attitudes in concert to provide not only content but form and
shape for her writing.

Undeniably influential among modernist writers, *Tender Buttons*
freed them from prescriptive notions of form and content. As William Carlos Williams said of Stein's influence, it was crucial because "writing, like everything else, is much a question of re-
freshed interest."[25] Stein's method for refreshing interest, at the
risk of trying patience simultaneously, was to use words subjectively. Randa Dubnick explains, "Stein had realized that words
need no longer be merely the means to the expression of another
reality, but may become freed of their normal mimetic function
(while still retaining their meanings and associations) and be used
plastically by the writer." She inverts the traditional descriptive
relationship of word to object: "Rather than the word evoking the
mental image of the object, the object evokes words that the writer
arbitrarily assembles into an independent linguistic object related

to, but not descriptive of, the model. . . . The writing no longer exists merely to describe the given object but becomes an entity in its own right."[26]

From poem to fiction, the complex writing known as modernism continuously tried to impress its readers that it was something new. Much of it stemmed from the basically poetic technique of concentrating meaning and emotion in an image. It therefore drew on premises that were essentially Bergsonian. As Bergson had written in his *Introduction to Metaphysics*, "The image has at least this advantage, that it keeps us in the concrete . . . many diverse images, borrowed from very different orders of things, may, by the convergence of their action, direct consciousness to the precise point where there is a certain intuition to be seized."[27] This new intuition, this relatively new way of apprehending, encouraged writers to accept the device of the image or scene as a means of making their perceptions fresh, clear, and immediate.

4

Modernism in 1925

With the publication of both T. S. Eliot's *The Waste Land* and James Joyce's *Ulysses* in 1922, the literary world found itself on notice that the "new currents of energy" Dos Passos described were permeating much recent literature. In America, what was taken to be Eliot's despair at the bleak impersonality of the technological, Godless culture, and the unredeemable chaos of postwar life, colored a number of literary depictions of the time. (As is often the case, writers were more likely to be influenced by writing than by what was happening in the surrounding culture: writers were responding to *The Waste Land* and less directly to America's temporarily prosperous milieu.) By 1925, a number of reactions to those key modernist texts were being published and, in their turn, discussed. A focus on 1925, one of the most interesting and important years of modernism, will allow us to see the various, and variant, literary currents of the period at its height.

One of the most fascinating books of that year was Ernest Hemingway's *In Our Time*, a collection of vignettes and stories. Hemingway had previously published very little—some poems and a few stories, the 1923 *Three Stories & Ten Poems*, and the 1924 *in our time*, the vignettes from this current book. He had, however, made friends with some of the central figures of modernism—Ezra Pound, Ford Madox Ford, Robert McAlmon, Gertrude Stein, James Joyce, Sylvia Beach, John Dos Passos, F. Scott Fitzgerald, William Carlos Williams, and others—and they helped to spread the word that this innovative and aggressive young American writer was someone to watch and read. Praised by Edmund Wilson and other literary critics, *In Our Time* became a sort of underground classic, making Hemingway one of the most sought-after writers of the 1920s.

What Hemingway achieved in his compilation of fiction was a striking means of making readers pay attention. Because one of the aims of the modernist was to make the process of reading fiction active, to involve the reader in the same way that reading poetry would, novels during these years were likely to be elliptical, spare, and highly concentrated. Readers were interpreters, who literally read and also simultaneously created the text. The intense concentration of event, image, symbol, character, and language meant that reading modernist texts involved their interpretation. The reader was forced to stop and ask, What is the significance of this detail? Why was that image chosen to open the narrative? Why was that line of dialogue placed there? What was the pattern of repetition that brought the single image into prominence?

When Hemingway assembled the collage of short stories and prose vignettes for *In Our Time*, he was fully aware of the effects he wanted to achieve. He had been sitting at the feet of Ezra Pound and listening to directions about the writer's responsibility to select and compose, thereby achieving a definite narrative intention. He had been listening as well to the advice of Stein, Joyce, Ford, and Fitzgerald. He may not have written a large quantity of prose by 1925, but what he had written had passed the test of helpful scrutiny by his friends, who also happened to be among the best writers of the age. Hemingway himself had written to Edmund Wilson that the effect he wanted to create in *In Our Time*—by alternating between the very brief vignettes about World War I and bullfighting, and the more formal stories, which were usually about a young man's life within his family and his marriage—was that of changing the focus of vision, "to give the picture of the whole between examining it in detail. Like looking with your eyes at something, say a passing coast line, and then looking at it with 15× binoculars."[1]

The brevity and intensity of the episodes, and their determination to strike the reader as directly as possible, made *In Our Time* appear to be amazingly new. The fact that these episodes also treated such difficult and unpleasant subjects as a boy's loss of faith in his father or a young man's bargain with God that he be allowed to live during wartime meant that the purpose of fiction had become as new as its style and form. In order to read *In Our Time* well, readers learned to start with the title of each piece and follow the image so created through the fiction. "The End of Something" seemed to be the story of an abandoned mill, but it became in its evolution the account of the break-up of a serious romance. "Cat in the Rain" appeared to be the somewhat inconsequential story of a young, homesick wife searching in the rainy Spanish night for a bedraggled cat, but it became the story of a young man's similarly bedraggled marriage and of his wife's loneliness as the result of his insensitivity to her. "The Doctor and the Doctor's Wife" emphasizes, at least in part, the classification of two adults in terms of what they do for a living. The doctor's self-consciousness about his prestige in the community interferes with his interaction with other men—here, with Native Americans who owe him money—and with his wife, a woman defined only by her marriage. The title suggests that the somewhat invidious strategies the doctor's wife has created to lead her life result from her social position as being only, or primarily, the doctor's wife. Modernist irony occurs when Hemingway stresses the fact that the doctor's wife (who is unnamed in the story) is a Christian Scientist and therefore does not believe in the efficacy of the practice of medicine. Some of the doctor's obvious frustration with his wife's reactions (imaged by his considering, even fondling, his loaded gun as he listens to her voice querulously invading his bedroom) surely stems from her philosophical resistance to his work.

Because every detail of Hemingway's seemingly casual stories and shorter prose pieces worked to create the total effect he intended, *In Our Time* became an apt illustration of the imagist/modernist aesthetic.

F. Scott Fitzgerald's *The Great Gatsby* was drawn from a similarly intense concern with craft, though readers who were familiar with his earlier novels and stories—*The Beautiful and Damned, Tales of the Jazz Age*—may not have realized the difference. (Of all the modernists, Fitzgerald had the largest popular following and was among the few modernist writers to live well on the income from his writing.) Decidedly more concentrated than his earlier fiction had been, *Gatsby* creates an intense fabric of linked scenes that ascribe almost symbolic—imagistic—significance to characters who, in themselves, seemed to represent stereotypical 1920s people. Through his friendship with Hemingway, Pound, and others of the modernist camp, Fitzgerald had become part of the new aesthetic scene. With his usual tendency to court approval, he was trying diligently to capture the new expression. *The Great Gatsby* can be read as an ambivalent answer to Eliot's *The Waste Land*, a text that does not deny the problems of modern culture that Eliot portrayed but one that presents characters who at least partly recognize some of the measures necessary to deal with those problems.

By telling the story of Jay Gatz, a poor young American bedazzled with the allure of wealth regardless of the way he achieved it, Fitzgerald epitomized the American dream of the early twentieth century: achievement as measured in possessions and position. By using Nick Carraway to narrate the Gatsby story, however, Fitzgerald was able to provide a grid for the reader's perceptions of that dream. Nick's skepticism about Gatsby's success leads the reader to question it while at the same time—because of the ambivalence Fitzgerald creates about Nick—questioning the reliability of Nick as narrator. The sympathy inherent in Gatsby's role—that the naive young boy would so singlemindedly scuttle whatever moral principles he had believed in, would pour his energy into becoming a figure without conscience or values—makes the narrative process complex enough to satisfy modernist readers who demanded intricacy. Sorting through the scenes that depict Gatsby as a romantic hero, who gives his devotion to the memory of his love for Daisy (regardless of what Daisy or his love has become) and works tirelessly toward the goal of recapturing both that love and the woman who was its object and icon, the reader is meant to sympathize with (even if not approve of) Gatsby. As intense as Fitzgerald himself was about his work as writer, so Gatsby earned his readers' respect because he embodied the American ethic of hard work, tenacity, and dedication. The irony of Gatsby's story was that his dream was faulty and that in the process of acquiring and achieving he eventually destroyed both his dream and himself.

Daisy's role in the novel is both ambivalent and ironic. Is she worthy of Gatsby's love, or does her betrayal of him warrant the reader's disapproval? Parallel with Nick's distance from Gatsby and his goals is Daisy's somewhat bewildered response to Gatsby's illicit but romantic courtship. What choice does she, finally, have? To adopt a life of much lower social standing—even of crime—by accepting Gatsby and relinquishing Tom or to salvage what she can from the episode and try to make a different kind of life with a man she has—perhaps wrongly—married. (Tom's racism and misogyny are emphasized early through his comments about white supremacy and through the contradictory value system that allows his affair with Myrtle, even while placing Daisy far above his mistress.

His physical brutality makes any acceptance of his character un-
likely, and yet Fitzgerald has created the situation so that either
Daisy remains faithful to her husband or she is herself reprehensible.) As Fitzgerald draws her, Daisy Fay's flaws are less directly her
own than they are the consequence of an economic system that has
made women—at least, women of middle and higher classes—
dependent for value on their marital state and on their physical
beauty. Daisy's final choice is reasonably defensible once the
reader considers women's position within the social and economic
milieu.

Fitzgerald's novel gains much of its effect not from these characters and their patterns of interaction but from the highly symbolic
scaffolding he creates throughout the book. The "wasteland" effect
of various landscapes Nick perceives as he—new to the area—
comments on either the bleakness or the corresponding lushness,
as at Gatsby's party, underlines the characters' almost desperate
searches for fulfillment. Wide gestures of extravagance, rushed
social engagements, frantic trips for pleasure (both the trip of Myrtle, Tom, and Nick into the city and the climactic journey of
Gatsby, Nick, Daisy, Jordan, and Tom on the day of what is to be
Myrtle's death illustrate the pace of these ill-at-ease questers): Fitzgerald does not rely on authorial intervention to explain the lives of
his creations but emphasizes in both plot and scene the malaise of
the affluent. *The Great Gatsby* is a busy novel, with much happening
in it. As such, it reflects the decade it is representing; the 1920s
were marked with the kind of energy that affluence makes possible
though as the often cynical Nick might have observed, little of the
activity "meant" anything.

The final effect of the novel is simply a mood of lost promise.
Gatsby had "made something" of himself but in so doing had
changed the self he could have become into the empty facade of an
unprincipled person. Fitzgerald's placing near the end the flash-
back to Jay Gatz's boyhood is a brilliant strategy. Once the reader
sees the pathetic list of moral principles from the boy's book, revealed even more pathetically by the father who has no capacity to
understand the tragedy in which his son has starred, the reader is
more likely to understand the trap of a highly romanticized ambition. Gatsby was as ephemeral as his false name—take a new one if
you do not like your family or your given "self"—and as likely to be
swayed by whatever whim he experienced. The influences of his

various friends (none of whom appeared at his funeral because they were so concerned with their own mortality) could therefore shape him dramatically. Gatsby's own vapid social gestures—in the cavalier scene when he pulls out the Christmas card in order to save himself a speeding ticket or during the incredibly long lunch that seems to exist mostly to allow Fitzgerald to make tasteless jokes about the Jewish Wolfsheim and his various body parts— show his decadent values.

Through each carefully chosen scene, Fitzgerald builds his indelible characters. We cannot forget any of them. Each serves as a catalyst for our own reactions, which shift and change as we read. Whether he knew how he had achieved it, Fitzgerald had written a deft and open text. It leaves room for readers to identify with one character or another, or with parts of one and parts of another, but also to withhold complete approval because of the conviction of reality. What results from reading *The Great Gatsby* is an ongoing dialogue with the characters. The reader wants to explain to Gatsby why he did not need to send the party guest a new dress, to Daisy why her daughter would not need to be a beautiful fool, to Jordan why she did not need to cheat at golf, and so on. The reading process has seldom been so active. Thoroughly "American" and modern in their fantastic dreams and their frenetic efforts to reach them, Fitzgerald's characters are also thoroughly American in their sometimes misguided aims.

Seemingly less modern in its style and technique, Ellen Glasgow's depiction of Dorinda Oakley in *Barren Ground* was one answer to Fitzgerald's portrait of Daisy (and to Hemingway's depiction of usually peripheral women characters in *In Our Time*, so peripheral that some readers forgot that there were women in Hemingway). In her characterization of Dorinda, Glasgow created a woman who met the problems of poverty, dependence, and sexual betrayal and rose above them. Dorinda's tactics were like Gatsby's—hard work, drive, devotion to her task—but they seemed much more positive in *Barren Ground*.

Written in a descriptive mode, Glasgow's novel relied more heavily on irony than her readers might have expected. The title itself suggested the opposite of the fruitful farm Dorinda created out of marginal land. The title was also gender specific: the barren woman had become another icon of the twentieth century because women were choosing whether to have the children that had previously been an expected, and accepted, part of marriage. In *Barren Ground*, Glasgow questioned both of these associations.

On the one hand, she created a single woman, at odds with both her family and the tradition in which she had been reared, able to work the field with hired laborers to bring marginal land to prosperity. On the other, her personal life seems barren because the child who would have been born from her illicit love with Jason Greylock was aborted after an accident. Glasgow's novel is a tribute to Dorinda's almost literal iron will, and the reader is less conscious of the character's lack of femininity than of that will. Dorinda does not seem, in any way, to be fruitless.

One of the most effective techniques Glasgow used in the novel was a modified stream of consciousness that related Dorinda's thoughts. Although most of the story is told through an omniscient narrator, some sections of Dorinda's narrative—particularly those relating to her love affair with Jason—occur in first person. Glasgow creates a broken, rhapsodic representation of her realizations. This departure from the omniscient narration used through most of the text calls attention to the change, and while the reader is focused so intensely on that section, more of Dorinda's character becomes explicable.

Understanding Dorinda is the main narrative problem. She appears to be a modern heroine, ready in the opening scene to quit her restrictive small town and find freedom. A strong if sheltered woman, Dorinda is beset by poverty, an unappreciative family (a contrary and contradictory mother, a repressive yet loving father, and a selfish brother who becomes a murderer before the novel's end), and a set of social expectations that rob her of autonomy and direction. Glasgow created a hero for the mid-1920s that spoke expressly to the feminist dilemma. Dorinda Oakley as Glasgow drew her was a character who wanted the protection and love of a family even though that family worked against whatever was best for her. She then came to want a relationship with a man who showed her largely duplicitous and double-standard behavior. Eventually she was asked to love him physically, only to be left carrying an unwanted child. Glasgow's portrait of Dorinda was admonitory: the so-called modern woman needed to have both strong direction and firm conviction that her acts are indeed hers, that she is behaving as she is because of what she intends and wants to accomplish.

In Dorinda Oakley's case, she appears at the beginning of the text as a victim of all kinds of conventions—her parents' and her culture's, the fascination with romance that makes her the dupe of Jason's attentions, and the underlying punishing ethic of her church that would turn her out and away once she is in trouble. The deus ex machina device of the accident after she has moved to New York City in search of anonymity frees her from the responsibility of the child, but Glasgow uses this loss to show that Dorinda also loses a large part of her humanity (her femininity and her sexuality) in the process. Unable to accept men's friendship after her love affair with Jason, Dorinda appears through the latter half of the novel as almost asexual.

There are many reasons for her self-protective shell, and Glasgow does a reasonably good job of portraying that shell as an accretion of years of mistreatment, chiefly psychological mistreatment. But the novel goes on too long. To have Dorinda finally marry Nathan, her good friend and the former husband of the woman she admired and cared for, and yet insist that his affection be completely platonic, changes her from the nurturing woman dedicated to reclaiming the barren land to some travesty of the supportive feminine. Nathan's heroic death during a train accident, and Dorinda's resulting remorse, intensifies the macabre aspects of their marriage. It is almost as if Glasgow needed an editor to tell her that the best parts of this novel were the intense early sections, and that once she began to write a lengthy and more nearly conventional novel (with loose ends neatly tied and reader's questions answered), she lost the power that her use of the more modernist traits of suggestion and ellipsis had already achieved.

As in Fitzgerald's *Gatsby*, in *Barren Ground* too the landscape of Dorinda's country, Virginia, conveys information about the circumstances of the hero. What is barren about the situation occurs repeatedly (and from the beginning of the text) in the image of the infertile broomsedge, "wave by wave, that symbol of desolation encroached in a glimmering tide on the darkened boundaries of Old Farm. It was the one growth in the landscape that thrived on barrenness."[2] To see only broomsedge wherever one looked was to mimic the heritage of the marginal farm. Hopeless, broken through the false idea that hard work can bring relief from poverty, Dorinda's father and mother reacted in different ways to their desolation.

By the end of the novel, both are dead, but the death of Dorinda's mother underlines forcefully the consequences of women's too altruistic choices. When Mrs. Oakley chooses to provide an alibi for the lying younger son, who is a murderer, she suffers a stroke. Ironically, it had been Dorinda's mother who had warned her daughter not to trust men: "You'll be all right married, daughter, if you just make up your mind that whatever happens, you ain't going to let any man spoil your life" (103). The sacrifice her mother makes by perjuring herself for Rufus shows Dorinda the futility of self-sacrifice. Although her mother knew the pitfalls of love, she could not refrain from defending the son she herself disliked. The barren world of Glasgow's making was a sphere in which men took and women gave and then lived as long as they did with the unforgettable consequences.

As complex as any other fiction of the 1920s, *Barren Ground* has been considered less than "modern" because its style seems full and explicit—perhaps because readers have not wanted to understand how ironic the author's presentations of characters are. Jason Greylock, the socially influential doctor, dies a pauper and a drug addict, his wife driven to suicide because (one supposes) of his treatment of her. She is the truly barren woman of the allusive title as she wanders the equally barren countryside in her madness, lamenting the imaginary deaths of children she never bore. In contrast, the comparatively unsophisticated Dorinda Oakley travels to the city, learns to appreciate and love music and the supposedly finer things, and returns to make something positive of her environs and her life. The reversal of reader expectation is a key modernist tactic.

Edith Wharton's *The Mother's Recompense* is another 1925 novel about a rebelliously strong woman character. Illustrating the premise that the years of modernism were also years in which readers were fascinated with the ways women characters lived and determined their lives—the working through of issues connected with the "new woman"—Wharton's novel deals with several controversial elements. Despite the title, being a mother has *not* been the central occupation of Kate Clephane, Wharton's protagonist. As a young wife and mother, Kate had run away with a lover, leaving her three-year-old daughter, Anne.

When the novel begins, Kate, in her mid-forties, is mourning the loss of Chris Fenno, her younger lover, from whom she has been separated six years. Her passionate affair with him followed the romance for which she left her husband and seems to have been in part a replacement for the fact that she had finally realized the cost of her running away: that she would never be allowed to see her daughter again. Her mourning is interrupted by a telegram from that daughter, inviting her back to America to live in the Clephane home now that her grandmother has died.

Because Kate has lived abroad all these years, no one in America knows anything about her past. Wharton's chief narrative strategy is to rely on the dramatic irony of the reader—through Kate—knowing what Kate's life has been, although her daughter, her daughter's guardian, and other family members know nothing. The pivotal narrative situation is that Anne wants to marry Chris, Kate's former lover, and the plot draws largely on ways Kate tries to prevent that marriage. The situation is complicated because Kate and Anne are much alike and care for each other deeply. By explaining her real objections to Fenno as a husband for Anne, Kate risks losing the daughter once more, and she also risks losing her regained place in the Clephane family, one that has pleasant social and financial benefits.

The fact is, as Wharton makes sure the reader knows, that Fenno has left Kate Clephane with no regard for the fact that she still loves him (there are moving flashbacks of Kate's pleading with him and his disinterested—even cold—responses), and therefore some of Kate's confusion about her feelings toward him stems from her own love. Could she live within a household and pretend that her daughter's husband had been a stranger to her? Wharton here works variations on the theme that she had used in earlier books, particularly *The Reef*, when Anna Leathe had to decide if she could marry a man who had been sexually involved with her future daughter-in-law. In Wharton's novels, the sanctity of the family is often pitted against the demands of passion, and part of her narrative method in her later novels is finding ways to make a character's struggle with these intensely private decisions vivid.

Wharton's fiction is never predictable, and in *A Mother's Recompense*, she sets up a possible marriage for Kate, only to have Kate herself break the engagement. Her decision remains mysterious, as if for Wharton, reasons were less interesting than actions. At the close of the novel Kate is living once more in Europe, happy in the knowledge that Anne has remained her daughter and loves her.

Kate faces a life of loneliness, but Wharton suggests that she is satisfied: "it had been her choice to fly as she had; and that in itself was a help."[3] The plot of the novel seems to discount its epigraph, which is Shelley's line, "Desolation is a delicate thing."

Kate Clephane—who has run away from a conservative and boring husband for a wealthy lover, who has then taken a much younger lover, who has lived even if marginally in an international milieu as a divorcee—is surely a "modern" female protagonist. The assumptions Wharton makes about the readers' response to this character are in themselves highly modern. Kate had left her only child, willingly, in her search for complete passion. That choice is hard to defend in most cultures, especially when the plot of Kate's later life is trying to come back into the daughter's life in a meaningful way. Wharton's choice of title seems to stress the centrality of Anne in Kate's life; the recompense of losing her lover is that she has her beloved daughter, and that same daughter now has the benefit of his love. Yet Wharton, with characteristic irony, gives the title more ambivalence that that. She dedicates the novel to the nineteenth-century British novelist Grace Aguilar and mentions that writer's influence on her grandmother. Aguilar wrote a novel titled *The Mother's Recompense*, a sequel to her 1847 fiction, *Home Influence: A Tale for Mothers and Daughters*. In both of Aguilar's novels, the character of Kate Clephane would have been most unwelcome. The contrast between the two novels carrying the same title made Wharton's irony clear. Kate Clephane's situation was not one that traditional women's wisdom could have prepared her for. It was unexpectedly, and embarrassingly, modern.

A more characteristic portrayal of women in twentieth-century times occurred in Anzia Yerzierska's 1925 novel, *Bread Givers*. Writing about the immigrant poor, in this case about the Russian Jewish community, Yezierska draws a damning portrait of the fathers who live entirely on the earnings of their uneducated, starved, and starving daughters—especially those who, having no dowry, will probably never marry. These women are, in effect, sold into the slavery of keeping their families—and when the fathers are educated and religious, as in the case of Sara Smolinsky's father, the paternal power of repression and guilt lasts the woman's entire life.

The irony of *Bread Givers* is that the paternal role of providing for a family almost always falls on the ill-equipped wife and the female children. When Mashah Smolinsky, the older sister and family beauty, marries a supposedly wealthy man, he maintains his own appearance and social life (buying new clothes, eating dinner in restaurants) while she lives penniless. When Sara visits her, Mashah can no longer beg milk from the milkman for her three children, lives in a hovel without lights, and has lost any vestige of her former beauty. Women's lives as Yezierska portrays them are dedicated to finding and procuring food, at a level of sheer subsistence. Sara herself sells stale herring for a penny profit; her mother rakes through piles of garbage; her sisters give their pitiful wages to the family without keeping anything for their own young lives. Yet within the family structure, their father, a rabbilike figure who has not worked in his adult life, eats well, lives in a separate room full of books (the rest of the family sleeps four to a bed in the main room of the house), and hardly notices the discomfort of the rest of the family. One of Yezierska's most touching leitmotifs is the mother bending over a kettle of soup, skimming off the fat and searching out the vegetables and meat for the father's meal, so that substantial food will nourish him. The working daughters and the mother eat the watery broth that remains.

Yezierska also ironically stresses the custom that women must marry to leave the paternal home, yet marriage is controlled largely by the father, whose own household needs their wages. None of the suitors the Smolinsky daughters choose for themselves is acceptable to their father because he does not at that time want to give up their incomes. Later he finds husbands for them, men who turn out to be depraved or liars but who have known how to play the game their father will respect. The sisters therefore marry, but live loveless—and in two cases, extremely impoverished—lives.

Yezierska makes clear through her insistent telling that the last thing their father considered was whether they would be happy. Clearly women's lot did not include happiness. It was to be a life of service, to children and to husband, ordered so that what continued was the family name. Scene after scene in *Bread Givers* depicts the terrible deprivation of women; one of the worst elements of the mistreatment of the Smolinsky children is the fact that their mother contributes to their misuse. Because she will not defy her husband's wishes, she cannot protect her daughters in any way. A victim herself, Yezierska intensifies her subjugation by pointing out that she had been very wealthy in Russia. Once married, she grew poor because her impractical husband lost *her* family's fortune. Coming to America was her husband's way of recouping their financial position: in America, so the legend went, everything was free. Again highly ironic is the case that this learned man had only false information.

Sara's way out of the imbroglio of her family poverty is to mimic her father and get an education. She goes to night school after a long day of ironing for subsistence wages, so that at the end of six years, she has a college degree and becomes a teacher. In order to get this education, she has lived on less than two dollars a week. She has given up seeing her family because she cannot afford the fare back to New Jersey. Ironically, once she graduates from college, she returns home to find her mother dying of gangrene. Had there been any medical attention, her mother would not have died.

The demands her father makes on Sara and her sisters after her mother's death seem inordinate, but the narrative Yezierska sculpts is convincing. Despite the hope that coming to America gives the women in this incredibly restricted culture, they never escape the guilt that their father's anger instills in them. Even as a self-supporting teacher, Sara feels that she has let her family down, that there should have been ways for her to share her minimal existence with them, to lighten the burden on her mother and sisters. After all, she had been lucky: she did not have to go to work until she was ten, and, as her imperious father often told her, other daughters had been working since they were six.

The irony Yezierska achieves by what seems to be simple reportage is almost unbearable. In one closing scene, Sara returns to her own meager room and berates herself: "My heart ached for Father. What was my duty? Was it to give my hard-earned school money to this woman healthy enough to go to work? If she married Father to have it easy was it not her own mistake? I tried to still my conscience with reason. But my heart ached with the unceasing question. What will become of Father if we abandon him to the mercy of that woman?"[4]

Even after Sara has married the school principal, Selig, she feels compelled to offer their home to her father: "I felt the shadow still there, over me. It wasn't just my father, but the generations who made my father whose weight was still upon me" (297). A poignant study of acculturation, of the boundaries of women's freedom despite their means of earning livelihoods, *Bread Givers* insists that culture itself must change. As trapped in her family and country heritage as she is in her father's words—"A woman without a man is less than nothing"—Sara carries within her deep patterns that intellectual understanding alone cannot change. For recording the complexity of a woman character's coming to some acceptance of life, this novel is unexpectedly sophisticated. It does not fall into the solipsistic trap of automatically equating life in America with new kinds of possibilities for women. For that discretion, as well as for her remarkably moving narration, Yezierska deserves a contemporary readership.

In some ways, John Dos Passos was also intent on depicting the lives of women in turn-of-the century America. *Manhattan Transfer* was, in draft, titled "Tess of 42nd Street," and the sometimes overlooked echoes of Thomas Hardy's novel *Tess of the D'Urbervilles* provide one key to what may seem a chaotic canvas of modern wasteland characters. Dos Passos was admittedly fascinated with urban existence, the sense of rush and turmoil that provided a tense backdrop for the lives and deaths of people caught up in achieving the American dream. For Dos Passos, women characters were as illustrative of that passion as were men—a pattern that continues through the *U.S.A.* trilogy.

Dos Passos opens *Manhattan Transfer* with the scene of Ellen Thatcher's birth, the baby squirming in a basket "feebly like a knot of earthworms."[5] The first chapter, titled "Ferryslip," includes as epigraph a prose poem about the garbage in the harbor as the ferry sails through it. Men and women leaving the ferry are, in the words of the author's heavily negative preface, "crushed and jostling like apples fed down a chute into a press" (3). Hardly an auspicious opening for either the novel or Ellen's life, these passages suggest that the journey about to be taken through Manhattan will be unpleasant at best. The irony of choosing a girl's life to show modern depravity marks Dos Passos's awareness of the problems of the new woman.

Other characters appear as the story continues: Bud Korpenning, on the run after murdering his father in upstate New York; Jimmy Herf, a Dos Passos–like character dependent on his beloved mother (who, in keeping with the somber tone of this text, dies shortly after she is introduced); Marcus Zucker, who cheats Ed Thatcher instead

of treating him to a drink as he had promised; Fifi Waters, the prototype of the scandalous actress; George Baldwin, the unscrupulous
lawyer. The list continues as the reader realizes that every character
and every scene adds some negative weight to the montage. Family
relationships, love relationships, business relationships are all dirt-
ied in this burgeoning metropolis. Dos Passos objects to the city's
reliance on appearance, its complete falsity, its disdain for human
life (the only happy character in the first part of the novel is the
firebug, observed by Ed Thatcher after he has lit a fire).

The modernist style of creating a work that readers need to identify with in order to read, of juxtaposing fragments of recognizable
"story" in random or imagistic order, is Dos Passos's method for
constructing *Manhattan Transfer*. After the numerous scenes and
characters have been introduced (some of the characters make only
a single appearance, so they contribute to mood rather than action), the narrative moves between events that concern Ellen
Thatcher and those that concern Jimmy Herf. Ellen, an actress and
the wife of a homosexual actor, lives in the same building as Jimmy
Herf's girlfriend. Once Herf and Ellen have come to know each
other, their paths continue to cross. The George Baldwin narrative
line also crosses theirs frequently. He finally falls in love with Ellen
and pursues her after her separation from her husband.

Dos Passos's text does not contradict the tone of Eliot's *The Waste
Land*, for whatever promise America has—*Manhattan Transfer*
suggests—is to be found outside its cities. When Jimmy Herf leaves
New York and Ellen, whom he has married overseas in the unreal
environment of war, he is running for freedom. Ellen turns into an
icy silhouette of the symbol of the modern, a New York skyscraper,
as she accepts George Baldwin's proposal of marriage. The reader
understands that because she is trapped in the culture's conventions
about women's behavior, she thinks she must marry—but the
reader also knows that her life will be unsatisfying, if not destroyed,
in this marriage. In contrast to Ellen's choice, Herf's leaving the city
and setting out to find himself is highly positive, a decision much in
keeping with those of nineteenth-century literary protagonists.

Willa Cather's *The Professor's House* seems to be a departure from
her novels about strong and often unappreciated women. In 1923
her *A Lost Lady* had told the story of Marian Forrester, an unconventional woman, searching within her role as wife to the much older,

venerable Captain Forrester for some vestige of personal, and sexual, satisfaction. The protagonists in Cather's 1925 novel, however—the professor whose family is moving into a new house as the result of income from his writing, and his former student, Tom Outland—are both male. The women to whom they entrust their lives and fortunes are described as ignoble products of the modern materialistic age, judging everything by its cost. In *The Professor's House,* Cather has created archetypal male figures to represent her own somewhat androgynous sympathies.

Professor St. Peter loves his work, which is research and writing. He lives a secret life among his papers and notes, hidden away in the third-floor attic, which is also a sewing room. Most of his life he has been able to keep his passion in check; people realized that he had to do this work as part of his professoriate. What they did not understand was that he could have done his university job well by just teaching. His research was his own intellectual passion.

Now that his multivolume history has made money, his wife and their two daughters think St. Peter should work less, should "enjoy" his life. They do not understand that his writing and his gardening have been the core of. his existence. When asked to move from their home into the newly constructed house that his earnings have made possible, St. Peter feels that he is being asked to leave the setting for his years of successful writing, as well as the garden he has constructed and cared for lavishly. Quietly, with his usual gentle stubbornness, he rents the old house back for a year, explaining that he needs to finish the project on which he is working. His intention is—whether or not he knows this consciously—that he will not move into the new house.

St. Peter's past life and its memories and his present existence coalesce through the novel's intermittent focus on the story of Tom Outland. Because Outland had been engaged to St. Peter's older daughter at the time of his death, he left to her his patents and his profits from an important invention. She and her current already-wealthy husband are spending much of the Outland money to construct and furnish a large estate to be known as Outland. St. Peter finds the project objectionable, even unfathomable. The Tom Outland he knew and loved was selfless. He would never have benefited in any personal way from his invention; he would never have called attention to his work. The Outland story that comprises the second section of the novel proves the temperament of this man, his nonacquisitive nature, beyond question, and shows how at odds he would have been with his former fiancée. Again working with clear modernist intention, Cather sets the Professor's story against the Outland story, and in her juxtaposition we see the similar characteristics.

The Professor is slowly turning into a stranger within his own family. They do not understand any of his motives or his actions. Tom Outland would have been given a similar reception once his selflessness became apparent. Cather's strategy is imagistic, and a few telling details chart the course of the entire novel.

Thinking about the death of Outland comes to have cataclysmic results when the Professor has time during a summer (his family is vacationing abroad) to consider how different he is from his wife and daughters. As a result of his realization, he comes close to suicide. He lives, however, and draws sustenance from the thought that he and Outland were the same kind of people, different from— and better than, in his value system—any other members of his family.

Cather's 1925 novel seems to be a logical extension of her countless narratives in which women's stories are told by male narrators. Here the artist figure—the person who lives with passion for work rather than for people—dominates the story. That in this case the artist figure is male, as is his student (better, disciple), means only that Cather finds the more interesting elements of that characterization to be asexual. Her identification with St. Peter is as complete as it was with Marian Forrester, gender aside. What she cares about in both St. Peter and Outland is their utter dedication to their work. Outland in his laboratory and in the Indian ruins, like St. Peter in his study, knew no life aside from that of the imagination.

In *Arrowsmith*, Sinclair Lewis's Martin Arrowsmith, a general practitioner who finally became the research physician he had always wanted to be, shared a number of St. Peter's traits. Neither Arrowsmith nor his mentor, the German scientist Max Gottlieb, fit into society: both are too dedicated to science and its nonmaterialistic ideals to be acceptable to the commercialism of the 1920s. Gottlieb, for all his indisputable brilliance, makes a number of bad career choices and ends his life in senility. He has been helpful, however, in giving Arrowsmith several chances to make important scientific discoveries, and those attempts give Lewis his narrative.

Gottlieb and Arrowsmith's wife, Leora, are his anchors as he tries general practice, more specialized medicine, and finally research.

Although Leora is an important character, Lewis often treats her—and their marriage—with levity. Only when Arrowsmith is coming into prominence after some years of marriage does Leora take center stage. When he plans to travel to Barbados to test a vaccine against the plague raging there, Leora insists on going with him. In her plaintive monologue, she sounds a great deal like Catherine in Hemingway's *A Farewell to Arms* (published four years later): "Don't you know I haven't any life outside of you? I might've had, but honestly, I've been glad to let you absorb me. . . . If you were off there, and I didn't know you were all right, or if you died and somebody else cared for your body that I've loved so—haven't I loved it, dear?—I'd go mad. I mean it—can't you see I mean it—I'd go mad! It's just—I'm you, and I got to be with you."[6] Ironically, it is Leora who dies—alone, while Arrowsmith contemplates an affair. Several critics have said that Leora is the most lifelike woman character Lewis drew, and *Arrowsmith* deserves to be read partly for her characterization.

The Barbados episode is the turning point in Arrowsmith's career. Instead of experimenting as he had planned, withholding the vaccine from all but those chosen for his research, Arrowsmith is so devastated by Leora's death that he indiscriminately vaccinates anyone who comes for treatment. Research becomes much less important than simply saving lives.

Conflicts between marriage and work test Arrowsmith, but he had conquered those until he married for a second time, to a very wealthy woman who soon decides she does not want to sacrifice her pleasure to science. Another more troublesome conflict in the novel is that between science and profit. Arrowsmith and Gottlieb leave positions when the pressure to make money demeans them. *Arrowsmith* ends somewhat predictably, with his giving up a chance to direct a research institute, leaving his second wife and their child to join forces with another scientist who had earlier left the competitive scene to work independently. In answer to Eliot's charge in *The Waste Land* that modern people had no sense of value or purpose, both Cather and Lewis were portraying people who lived wholeheartedly for their work, and in each case, their work benefited all of society. Readers evidently sided with Lewis in his belief because *Arrowsmith* was one of the best sellers of 1925.

Theodore Dreiser was also fascinated with the lives of young men who aspired to the conventional American dream, that of success and prosperity, and marriage to a beautiful woman as an external symbol of that success. In *An American Tragedy*, Dreiser told the story of the inexperienced and earnest Clyde Griffiths, whose sudden chance at all the elements of the dream demolished any moral understanding he might have had. Working as he frequently did from actual life, in this case from the sensational Chester Gillette murder trial of 1906, Dreiser involved his readers with the pathos of Griffiths's ambition: to rise from poverty, to find someone to love, and to find happiness.

Unfortunately, when Griffiths does find someone to love, she (Roberta Alden) becomes pregnant. Because she is only a shop girl and by that point in his hegira toward success, Clyde is also dating the rich and beautiful Sondra Finchley, he thinks of killing Roberta. When he has taken her to a lonely lake, as if on their way to marry, his intention changes; but in the meanwhile their boat tips and Roberta drowns. Intentionality is the key, and the second half of the book, Clyde's trial, deals with issues of moral responsibility. The immense carelessness of the rich, shown earlier in scenes similar to Fitzgerald's in *The Great Gatsby*, becomes one theme, alongside the perverse lack of moral strength Griffiths's life illustrates so well.

An American Tragedy is usually considered a text of the late naturalist movement, another illustration of the human being at odds with society because of an incomplete understanding of personal and social values—the human organism responding almost as if it were animal. Yet taken in relation to other novels of the 1920s, it shows the same kinds of dilemmas and the same possibilities of resolution. It therefore becomes less naturalistic than it is modernist in that Griffiths is truly a lost man, depending for part of his philosophy on wealthy and shortsighted relatives, for another part on his own poorly educated family, and for a third, on the media, which represent the culture of the time. Griffiths "thinks" exactly what is written in the newspapers. Part of the fascination of following his behavior after Roberta's death is the degree to which it mirrors the newspaper coverage of that event, including his role in it. The "universal" nature of Griffiths's crime is made clear in Dreiser's choice of *An* rather than *The* in his title.

Although most of the text focuses on Clyde Griffiths, some attention is given to Roberta, and in her situation—as in those of Carrie Meeber or Jennie Gerhardt in Dreiser's earlier novels—the author proves that he knows and understands women characters, especially those trapped in poverty. In this novel as in many others of the 1920s, sexual knowledge is both a way out of personal inhibition and despair and a way into tragedy, especially in the eyes of society. Just as Martin Arrowsmith and Leora felt the condemnation of small-town society in *Arrowsmith* and Kate Clephane felt it from the higher reaches of society in *The Mother's Recompense*, so Dreiser's characters suffer punishment more frequently than enlightenment in their sexual exploration.

An interest in the sexual pervaded much of the writing of Sherwood Anderson as well, particularly during the 1920s. He was also fascinated by the narrative presentation of the sexual dilemma (how could the writer deal with the topic and yet not have his work banned?), just as he was searching for ways to show that the sexual and psychological basis for character was the heart of most fiction. In *Dark Laughter*, Anderson grouped characters together on the basis of their understanding of sexuality in what appeared to be the common modernist plot: the search for meaning. Whenever Anderson chose to write a novel, he was burdening himself technically; most readers agree that he was the true master of the short story. Achieving organic form, shape and tone congruent with action and character, was his strength; and sustaining a form appropriate to everything happening in an entire novel was usually beyond his skill. While readers awaited his collections of stories, Anderson's novels often met with critical hostility.

Dark Laughter was one of his best-selling novels, however, partly because it told several different stories. The plot line was consequently more interesting than that of some of his earlier fictions, and the fragmented text, pieces of one narrative interposed with sections of another, moves quickly. As usual with Anderson, lead characters were men: Sponge Martin, Bruce Dudley, Fred Grey. Their fascination was with women, and some of the novel takes place in Paris, where people are recovering from the war and living life to the fullest. Sensual scenes, serious flirtations, a sequence of divorces and good marriages are linked through the somewhat random plot connections. Much of the sexual experimentation takes place in France and echoes what Anderson appears to consider a more honest American sexuality, that found among blacks. The "dark laughter" of the title occurs when blacks are talking and laughing together, often about the foibles of their white employers. Such laughter signals transgressions as well as the revelation of honest passion. Anderson's use of the modifier *dark* is more than a racial signifier; it taps into the repressed and conflicted view of open sexuality prevalent among most readers (and writers) of the time.

The central plot line concerns both Sponge Martin, whose love for his wife continues after many years of marriage, and Fred Grey, who meets a strange young American woman during a visit to Paris. He proposes when they have known each other only a few hours. Once Aline has married Grey and returned from Paris to live in the small Indiana town where the family's manufacturing plant is located, she forgets her European knowledge and becomes a midwestern wife. But when she sees Bruce Dudley, an employee in her husband's factory, sexual attraction draws her to him. The remainder of the novel deals with Aline's almost unconscious plot to ensnare Dudley.

Once she and Dudley have become lovers (a single episode, with no language involved, or so Anderson presents the scene), Aline becomes pregnant. She tries to live as Fred's wife, pretending the child is his (Dudley has immediately left town). But when she is several months away from delivery, her lover returns, and they quickly understand that they must be together. Although Fred thinks of murdering them, or at least Dudley, or perhaps one of the laughing black women in his employ, his threat of violence is futile. He too is lulled by the strange complacency that Anderson's *Dark Laughter* emanates. Whether it is sexual complicity, as in the case of Sponge Martin and his wife and Bruce and Aline, or simple reverence for the mystery of the sexual, as in Fred's history, the pervasive effect of Anderson's narrative is that of fated involvements.

Anderson achieves the effect of unintentionality by using sentences that are incomplete: "Sponge the workman telling old Grey to go to hell, offering to kick him out of his shop. . . . A bonfire down near the river's edge. Catfish lines out." Just as random are the narrative lines in the story, with an opening that deals with Dudley and Sponge, switching for little reason to some friends of Aline so that eventually she can be introduced. A central character midway through the novel is the flamboyant journalist who longs to experience everything sexual—Rose Frank, who "danced with a man who tore her dress open." As Rose told about the Quat'z Arts Ball, her listeners were as intrigued with her state of mind after being there as they were with her stories about it: "The pantomimes began at twelve, Rose said—twenty-nine ways of lovemaking—all done in the life—naked people. There was a moment. At twelve any woman who wanted to save herself could get out. After that all barriers down. 'I stuck.' "[7] What Anderson achieves is almost artless, the sense of narrative ordered for no purpose, language accumulating as if someone were speaking to friends. What coheres is the language around an image, and in this case, the title image of dark laughter, representing the all-knowing, and all-responding, sexuality of various people.

William Carlos Williams's collection of essays about American culture—rather, about the "heroes" from that culture—titled *In the American Grain* and based in part on D. H. Lawrence's *Studies in Classic American Literature*—also appeared in 1925. Williams's readers were accustomed to thinking of him as a poet, so their response to this book disappointed him, but he was firmly committed to the anti-Puritan view of history he had created in the text.

Williams felt that the harshly restrictive treatment of the Other, of the different, in American culture was the country's greatest weakness (part of his feeling stemmed from the fact that he was half–Puerto Rican and well aware of his own difference). He identifies with such historic figures as Eric the Red, Columbus, Daniel Boone, and Lincoln and champions them for their imaginations and their courage as explorers. Part of the mystique of the discovery of America is a feminine model, what Williams calls the "female principle," and in that image he combines eros and agon, the power of the imagination with the sensual. Just as de Soto was fascinated by rivers, so others of Williams's characters taken from history were attracted by the sexual. Geography became the way to a full appreciation of the more intimate regions that sexuality suggested, just as in Williams's later five-book epic poem, *Paterson*, the land of his chosen area of New Jersey came to represent the individual understanding and consummation of the poem's hero, Dr. Paterson.

In the American Grain has become a classic, partly because its sentiments caught the mood of the time and partly because each of its essays was written in a different style and structure. The essay collection is a textbook for organic form, shape suited to content. As Williams recalled in his *Autobiography*, "The Tenochtitlan chapter was written in big, square paragraphs like Inca masonry. Raleigh was written in what I conceived to be Elizabethan style; the Eric the Red chapter in the style of the Icelandic saga; Boone in the style of Daniel's autobiography; Franklin was in Franklin's words; and John Paul Jones I gave verbatim. Thus I tried to make each chapter not only in content but in the style itself a close study of the theme."[8] The book also posed questions about the differences between literature and history and the importance to the creative mind of having a base of historical information. It contributed to the ongoing dialogue between writers who attempted to mirror life (the so-called realists and naturalists, those who wrote local color works or novels of manners) and those who tried to create their own fictional worlds (the Impressionists, the lyric novelists, the more radically avant-garde). Williams held a central position within the community of writers from the early 1920s, though he was less well known among general readers.

Gertrude Stein's position was similar. Few writers were so important to other writers, yet it was not until the 1930s—with the publication of *The Autobiography of Alice B. Toklas*—that Stein found a wide readership. When *The Making of Americans* was published in 1925, after some sections of it had appeared in Ford Madox Ford's *transatlantic review*, little attention was given to the immense and confusing text.

The source book for Stein's views of the efficacy of repetition, the long novel dealt with the most American of subjects (though Stein had for twenty years or longer been living in Paris), the formulation of the American character. The novel was a culmination of much of Stein's earlier work. Though she changed family names, many of the characters in this text had grown from earlier novellas such as *Fernhurst*, *Q. E. D.*, and the "Melanctha" novella from *Three Lives*. As Leon Katz points out in his chronology of Stein's early writing, she had begun writing what was to be this 1925 novel before anything else in her oeuvre, probably as early as 1902. Therefore it is more accurate to say that *The Making of* was Stein's early work than that it grew from that early writing. Through the evolution of her finished text (probably in 1911, with the book then lying dormant until Hemingway used parts of it in the journal), she wrote and rewrote, brought in sections that were to find audience in other prose, and redefined her concepts of the immediate present, character (complete with the necessary "sense of human struggles"), and the important function of narrative to show the unfolding of human personality, whether or not that unfolding resulted in observable "action."[9]

The Making of Americans was originally to tell the story of one American family, but it soon grew to two families, their primary and peripheral characters giving Stein the opportunity to focus on character types crucial to her (her first lover, the antagonist for that relationship, family members, herself in several roles) and those that were commonplace in American turn-of-the-century life. In her writing, the fairly conventional moral Stein seemed intent on showing—that women should stay within their patriarchal social orders and welcome the protection available there, especially avoiding bad marriages—itself changed until the expected became the criticized. Stein's text became a means for her to sort through her own contradictory experiences and decide what kind of writer, as well as what kind of person, she was to be. The novel is both a culmination and a model, drawing in a number of theories about ways to show personaltiy while at the same time showing other writers how much could be achieved in an almost plotless narrative. And because of Stein's reliance on repetition and on the commonplace phrase, few readers saw how much of a debt she owed to Henry James—despite the obvious philosophical connections among the three (Henry James as writer, Stein as writer, and Stein also as student of William James, Henry's influential brother, the seminal psychologist of the nineteenth century).

Grouping William Carlos Williams and Stein with innovative poets such as H.D. whose Collected Poems appeared in 1925, and Robinson Jeffers, whose poems in Tamar combined the immediate and the mythic, and several black writers (Alain Locke, whose essay collection The New Negro focused the Harlem Renaissance, Countee Cullen, whose poem collection Color was as heavily sensual as Anderson's Dark Laughter, and Jessie Redmon Fauset whose 1924 novel There Is Confusion was among the most important fiction of the Renaissance) with such playwrights as Eugene O'Neill and John Howard Lawson allows the reader to sense those currents of energy Dos Passos had earlier mentioned. Reading an avant-garde journal during the mid-1920s was exciting: nothing was predictable, everything was possible, and—most important of all—every word written was considered a meaningful aritistic experiment. American writing in 1925 was both defining and describing not only a key decade but American culture at one apex of its maturity. Writers believed that what was happening in America was of interest to the whole world, and they wrote accordingly. American literature in 1925 was a statement of difference, a glimpse of possibility, and a window to the future.

5

Crosscurrents: Paris and Harlem

Many of these important books published in 1925 were written by American authors who were at least temporarily living outside the United States. Gertrude Stein had lived abroad for more than twenty years, Edith Wharton for more than a decade. Ezra Pound, after trying to cope with a British imperialism more idiosyncratic than his own, had moved to Paris, where with Ford Madox Ford, William Bird, and Robert McAlmon he attempted to establish alternate publishing avenues for himself and his friends. Sherwood Anderson, F. Scott Fitzgerald, John Dos Passos, Claude McKay, e. e. cummings, Sinclair Lewis, William Faulkner, Nathanael West, Thomas Wolfe, Stark Young, Ernest Hemingway, Waldo Frank, Harry and Caresse Crosby, Hart Crane, Langston Hughes, Malcolm and Peggy Cowley, Man Ray, Gerald and Sara Murphy, Jessie Fauset, Alain Locke, and Edmund Wilson were frequent visitors to Paris; and H.D., Sylvia Beach, Margaret Anderson, Janet Flanner, Djuna Barnes, and other women writers settled with alacrity in either Paris or London. To become an expatriate was to join a long tradition of American writers, beginning with James Fenimore Cooper and Washington Irving and continuing to Henry James and T. S. Eliot— writers who often found that they had a greater grasp on the essential American experience by being at least temporarily removed from it. As Hemingway had written in *A Moveable Feast*, "Maybe away from Paris I could write about Paris as in Paris I could write about Michigan."[1]

The point of expatriation early in the twentieth century seemed to be not to come closer to the country from which one ran but rather to run, and to find something different in the running. As Janis P. Stout suggests in her study of the journey narrative, the American writer's expatriation is often an escape from the country. The force is "propulsive"; the journey is not a journey *toward* but a journey *away from,"* and taking it is a victory, a means of escaping the social prison America has come to be.[2] Malcolm Cowley disagrees, assessing modernist expatriation as a search for "a spiritual home" rather than exile.[3] For some writers, the positive search may have outweighed the motive of escape, but for most writers, the elements were surely mixed. Man Ray speaks to the normalcy of living in Paris: "Everything about the place struck me as being just about right. I had the feeling that this was the best possible place in the world for the artist to live and work; and at the time it was. There was so much of the past and the immediate present brought together on one plane that nothing seemed left to be desired. And there was no feeling of being isolated from America."[4]

Paris was "the best possible place in the world for the artist" at least partly because it allowed a variety of life-styles and sexual arrangements. American homophobia was one of the reasons H. L. Mencken denounced its "booboisie" so vehemently. Shari Benstock in *Women of the Left Bank* points out that life-styles that could never have been tolerated in the United States were accepted in France and that freedom from restrictive social, sexual, and legal codes was one great attraction of life abroad.[5] It was much more than the legendary sexual freedom, availability of liquor, and the lower cost of housing and food—though these considerations were important as well. It was the sense of unrestricted openness to new ideas, new practices, new aesthetic principles, and new ways of understanding the human mind, as well as the human condition. In Virgil Thomson's words, life in Paris during the 1920s was a "joyous season."[6]

One of the most consistent attributes of modernist writers was their sense that living in America—at least in white, middle-class America—was not the way to develop their talents or to fulfill their ambitions. When the sales of Sinclair Lewis's 1920 novel *Main Street* topped 300,000 in its first year and continued strong, social observers knew the "revolt from the village"—and the repression that village life implied—was in full swing. Living in the circumstances they had known in rural or small-town America was not going to mesh with the kind of work young artists wanted to do. The prototype of the alienated artist applied to nearly all modernist writers, and the exodus to Europe throughout the twentieth century graphically testified to what artists considered their disenfranchisement, their difference from mainstream America.

One alternative to traveling to Europe was living in New York City's Greenwich Village. Many young writers and artists opted for that choice, particularly in the immediate postwar years—Edna St. Vincent Millay, Mabel Dodge, Carl Van Vechten, Max Eastman, Hutchins Hapgood, Louis Untermeyer, John Reed, Stuart Davis, Lloyd Dell, Edmund Wilson, and others who returned once Europe had lost its attraction. In close touch with the publishing world (and the important new publishers Huebsch, Harcourt, Knopf, and Liveright, influential both in publishing new writers and, in the case of Liveright, fighting the censorship of the Society for the Suppression of Vice and the 1923 Clean Books Bill), Greenwich Village residents felt themselves in the vanguard of the new art. Next to the Village, the most interesting section of New York was Harlem, where the famed Harlem Renaissance in black art occurred from 1915 through the early 1930s. In some ways, the American modernist fascination with black culture and arts— music, writing, painting—may well have been part of the same attitude that led to expatriation: nothing that was acceptable, and accepted, in mainstream America could possibly be useful to the incipient modernists. Only the unfamiliar, the exotic, the primitive could trigger truly new responses in the artist's imagination. Black culture became important in both Paris and America, benefiting from an unfeigned interest among white publishers and intelligentsia in black music (particularly jazz), art, and poetry and fiction. Once a market existed for black art and literature, there was a great deal available to choose from.

Evidence of the attraction of European, and especially French, culture appears in modernist literature obliquely but consistently. In Dos Passos's *Manhattan Transfer*, Paris becomes the land of Jimmie Herf's dream as he marries Ellen Thatcher and they have a child. (Once back in the United States, that dream turns to nightmare, and the marriage crumbles. In the United States, Paris appears to be a place to buy liquor—little more.) In Anita Loos's *Gentlemen Prefer Blondes*, travel is exotic and freeing, and in Conrad Aiken's *Blue Voyage*, the journey itself is the excitement. France is a source of peace and comfort in many of Edith Wharton's novels, as when Ellen Olenska returns to Paris to live in *The Age of Innocence*.

For H.D., too, Paris is alluring and exciting, but her characters only visit. In Fitzgerald's *Tender Is the Night*, foreign culture provides the only possible environment in which the Divers might manage to exist. Gertrude Stein's *The Autobiography of Alice B. Toklas*, published in 1933, was a paean to Paris. Only the first few pages of the book do not deal with life abroad, and the beginning of chapter 2—"This was the year 1907. . . . The home at 27 rue de Fleurus consisted then as it does now of a tiny pavillon of two stories with four small rooms, a kitchen and bath, and a very large atelier adjoining"—is the real beginning of the book.[7] In Toklas's voice, Stein tells the somewhat romanticized—and self-praising—story of living in the midst of the Paris art scene.

William Carlos Williams's *A Voyage to Pagany* (1928) probably catches more accurately than most other accounts the sense of difference that living in Europe creates for the middle-class American. Williams was working from actual experiences he had had on several trips to Paris during the mid-1920s. (Though he lived in New Jersey and had a medical practice there, he and his wife, Flossie, took two years off— during one of which they left their two boys with friends and a maid—in order to find out what the immense attraction of Europe was. Their need to explore Europe and the artistic scene there, even at the cost of Williams's practice, suggests how important being in Paris had become to any aspiring American writer.) As Williams recalled in his *Autobiography,* "*Everyone* was in Paris—if you wanted to see them. But there were grades too of that cream."[8]

For Dev Evans, Williams's protagonist in *A Voyage to Pagany,* Paris provided new experiences, largely sexual, and a new definition of himself as an American. The simple plot—with Evans meeting different women sequentially and learning from each of them— emphasizes his process of defining himself, the real reason for his quest. Through encounters with men who are artists; with the young virgin Bess—about to become the lover of a European, an echo of a Jamesian motif of the American innocent perverted by the experienced European; with Fraulein von J. who plans to enter a convent rather than live in America; with the musician Grace Black, and—most important to the novel—with the statue of the Venus, Evans comes to understand that he is, indeed, a naif, an innocent American who must soon return to the country that so frustrates him. Even as he recognizes that in his country, honor has become "starved, thin, lying," he still understands that it *is* his country, and as he returns home, with the coast of Maine in sight, he says, "So this is the beginning." Part of Williams's attraction for Paris may have stemmed from his work translating Philippe Soupault's novel, *Last Nights of Paris* (*Les Dernières nuits de Paris*), in which the discreet whore, Georgette, symbolizes the mysteries of the city. Impressionistic and highly fragmented, the Soupault novel is a montage of color and emotion, with little explicit plot or characterization. What remained for Williams was the compressed image of a city like a woman, a place becoming person—the kind of metaphor he would create in *Paterson*.

None of these books was published before Hemingway decided to use the expatriate experience as the basis of his fiction. Considering how often he and his friends must have commented on the naturalness of that topic and how committed they had become to their European life-style, the absence of more fiction about living abroad is noteworthy—unless one assumes that many of the expatriates were spending their energies living rather than writing or had become frequenters of bars where writers went to be seen rather than to work. By the time Hemingway had published *In Our Time* and was looking for a subject for a novel (of his friends, only he had not written one), a fiction about Paris, a group of expatriate Americans and British, and the strange alliances that travel and displacement could create seemed the answer. For several years he had been working with Spanish bullfight material in the vignettes of both *in our time* and *In Our Time*, so he knew his novel would include Spain. But the impetus for *The Sun Also Rises* is more directly life in Paris and what Jake Barnes has learned through living there. Hemingway's emphasis on Paris gives the novel its tone, through its comparatively long introductory scenes, and helps to establish the ways fiesta time in Spain differs from a more commonplace Paris life.

From the earliest scenes with Robert Cohn, foil for most of Jake's views, Hemingway uses attitudes about place to show the difference between the two. Jake advises Robert calmly, when he insists that they go to South America, "This is a good town. Why don't you start living your life in Paris?" To all Cohn's arguments, Barnes says only, "Wasn't the town nice at night?"[9] The serenity, the sense of being able to be oneself, makes Paris ideal for Jake—and subsequent scenes with Georgette and Brett, as well as alone, reinforce that image of freedom. Jake had also told Robert that, on the one hand, place is immaterial: "Going to another country doesn't make any difference. I've tried all that. You can't get away from yourself by moving from one place to another" (12). But he also knows that place is important as a surrounding, as a location in which to live and work—rather than as escape. Given that Jake will be Jake no matter where he is, he chooses to live in Paris—and to spend his summers in Spain.

When Bill Gorton appears, Jake creates an American alliance, setting himself and Bill against the apparently more cosmopolitan (but actually weaker and more erratic) British. Hemingway shows the depth of their friendship through much of the humor that exists in the novel, and as Scott Donaldson has pointed out, Bill's humor is both wise and contagious. Bill, modeled on Hemingway's friend, Donald Ogden Stewart, "directs jibes at ideas and institutions, not human beings. In this way, Gorton provides a model of behavior that—unlike the code of the intrepid Romero—it is possible to emulate. 'I did not care what it was all about,' Jake reflects in one of his interior monologues, 'All I wanted to know was how to live in it' (p. 148) Gorton seems to have discovered how: without Jake's bitter sarcasm, without Mike's and Brett's disingenuous self-depreciation, without Robert's self-pity, with the best will in the world."[10] And as Donaldson also makes clear, the dialogue between Bill and Jake is thoroughly American in language, attitudes, and tone.

Much of the commentary about America is critical, of course, but Hemingway seems to be willing to set America's problems against those so obvious in Europe. Jake Barnes has made his choice and his choice is to live in Paris; there is no ambivalence about that. Yet he cannot remove himself entirely from what happens in America because it is his country; references to the Scopes trial, to current reviewers in American magazines, to American writers, and to American attitudes pepper the novel. There is no question that *The Sun Also Rises* is written by an American. Some of the less obvious irony occurs, in fact, when Brett attempts to link herself with Jake, presuming on their love to make her a compatriate. When she says to Count Mippipopolus that he is "one of us," the reader knows how wrong she is. The count, with his broken English, has little in common with Jake Barnes, and the comparison makes the reader question just how much Brett understands about her American lover. Later scenes in the novel underscore that difference, especially when she and Jake visit the bullring and the church. Brett can

absorb some of what happens in the bullring, but without a comple-
mentary religious experience, her comprehension of the bullfight is
limited. That she and Jake are living their lives from different moral
bases is clear long before the closing scene. It is important, however, that Hemingway made that closing scene as clear as it is
because the difficulties of reading this expert modernist—and often
elliptical—novel meant that numerous interpretations of both character and event exist.

The Sun Also Rises led readers to consider Hemingway the ideal
modernist: fresh subject matter, fresh stylistic devices, fresh insights. The book answered Eliot's The Waste Land clearly as it
showed that characters could both endure and learn from their war
experiences. Not everything was gone; even the most shattered
characters (Jake, with his injury; Brett, with her damaged psyche)
had survived, and survived well. In fact, it could be said after
reading The Sun Also Rises that for some characters, the war had
created moral values.

By approaching his theme from the perspective of the expatriate,
however, Hemingway made that understanding much more difficult to assume. Fitzgerald's Gatsby was the instructive American
novel, through which readers could judge their own morality and
empathy. Fitzgerald could call into question some of the verities that
Sinclair Lewis was drawing as fact in Main Street and Babbitt and
know that his readers would appreciate his skepticism. Hemingway's Sun was the instructive American expatriate novel, through
which readers could locate their own morality. In the process of
reading Hemingway's text, readers began with critical attitudes toward America (the epigraph of Stein's calling the postwar crowd "a
lost generation") and then came into a more complete understanding of the country (the juxtaposition of the calming passage from
Ecclesiastes). The latter reasonably affectionate view was possible
because Hemingway brought the reader to see through the eyes of
Bill Gorton and Jake Barnes. Typical of the best modernist texts, The
Sun Also Rises was a difficult and an ambiguous book, but it was a
very American one as well.

The Sun Also Rises is the text that grew at least partly out of the
high-spirited defiance Hemingway felt as he lived abroad. Not
quite so adolescent as was his epigraph to his 1924 in our time ("Tell
us about the French women, Hank. What are they like? . . . How
old are the French women, Hank?"), Hemingway's first novel tried

to preserve the exhilaration of that life in Paris, the life he was to remember longingly when, almost at the end of his by-then tortured life, he composed the vignettes that made up *A Moveable Feast*.[11] "There is never any ending to Paris," Hemingway writes at the close of his memoirs. "We always returned to it no matter who we were or how it was changed or with what difficulties, or ease, it could be reached. Paris was always worth it and you received return for whatever you brought to it" (211). It is that spirit of love and commemoration that *The Sun Also Rises* captures so effectively.

There were a number of kinds of expatriation, however, and some of the most significant modernists persisted in writing only about America, and about small segments of it. Much modernist fiction reflects a kind of expatriation of the imagination, none so obvious as that provided in the fiction of Thomas Wolfe. Although Wolfe did not return often to his North Carolina environs, particularly once *Look Homeward, Angel* had been published in 1929, his writing seldom left that location. It was as if his imagination had burrowed in behind the mountains—or, perhaps more accurately, as if all that mattered about a person's story was to be found in that single, intimate location and the relationships among people that lived there. William Faulkner followed something of the same pattern, creating and embroidering his little postage stamp of Mississippi soil, naming it Yoknapatawpha County, dividing its acres, peopling it, and absorbing all the knowledge possible from both its terrain and its inhabitants. Both writers were drawing on the important achievement of Sherwood Anderson, when he had given life to his postage stamp of Ohio soil in *Winesburg*.

This detailed localism was also the pattern followed by Jean Toomer, when he created the 1923 montage text he called simply *Cane*. The impetus for much of Toomer's writing, both poetry and prose, came from his visit to Sparta, Georgia, where he saw and lived an entirely different kind of life from that he was accustomed to in the more sophisticated Washington, D.C. As Toomer wrote to the *Liberator*, "A visit to Georgia last fall was the starting point of almost everything of worth that I have done. I heard folk-songs come from the lips of Negro peasants. I saw the rich dusk beauty that I had heard many false accents about, and of which till then, I was somewhat skeptical. And a deep part of my nature, a part that I had repressed, sprang suddenly to life and responded to them. . . . My point of view has not changed; it has deepened, it has widened."[12] Born of several different racial lines, Toomer was never comfortable being described as black, but when *Cane* was published, its author was so identified and his work praised as the writing of a black author.

Cane was in some ways as influential in 1923 as Anderson's *Winesburg, Ohio*, had been in 1919. Its precise yet densely imaged short stories and poems were heavily sexual and mysterious, often about southern black women. All the taboo subjects and innuendoes of Waldo Frank's *Holiday* and *The Dark Mother* and James Branch Cabell's *Jurgen: A Comedy of Justice* appeared in such beautifully shaped poems and vignettes that no modernist could fault them. "Karintha," refrains from songs juxtaposed with sensual descriptions of her dusky beauty, opens the evocative text: "Men had always wanted her, this Karintha, even as a child, Karintha carrying beauty, perfect as dusk when the sun goes down."[13] Open vowels, accented with hard *k* sounds, suggest the soft pliancy of the female body, as does the sentence structure, which begins with *Men*, who act, and act on the objective woman who only carries beauty. Karintha is not an actor; she does not create anything. Such expert use of syntax, rhythm, and language marks most of the short fiction and poems in this collection, though each piece varies widely in tone.

The directness of "Becky" makes her story quietly horrible (she dies in a fire, after the town has abandoned her because she, a white woman, has borne children by black fathers), and Toomer's terse language accurately creates the town's censure: "Becky had one Negro son. Who gave it to her? Damn buck nigger, said the white folks' mouths. She wouldn't tell" (14). "Fern" describes another lush and unapproachable woman, but its irony is that part of her alienation from her black culture comes from her Jewish "blood." "Carma" does fit into her culture, almost too well, because she has many lovers, and much of her lovemaking occurs in the cane. She also hides there when her angry husband searches for her. "Wind is in the cane," an eerie refrain, suggests the macabre happenings that occur because, as Toomer writes explicitly, "Time and space have no meaning in a canefield. No more than the interminable stalks" (11).

Linked through the image of cane—with its suggestion of sweetness, phallic shapes, earthy produce, commonality, dense cover, and the oblique reference to the biblical Cain with its entirely different context—these stories unite to form a cohesive whole. Yet they are also brilliantly varied, as language conveys the specific tone of Toomer's design. His poems are even more interesting, ranging from free form to regular stanza, from bitter mockery ("Her Lips Are Copper Wire. . . . with your tongue remove the tape / and press your lips to mine / till they are incandescent" [54]) to Whitmanesque praisesong ("I am a reaper whose muscles set at sundown. All my oats are cradled" [69]). Other repeated images lace the works together—wind, sun, dusk, pine, fire, water, ash, eyes, lips—and the variation Toomer achieves, working from his severely limited focus, is impressive. The text begins as if the writer were observing women in the South, creating narratives of their lives, but that observational format is widened through a variety of poems—from those about the land and its products to such sardonic accounts as "Conversion" or the sobering "Portrait in Georgia":

> Hair—braided chestnut,
> > coiled like a lyncher's rope,
> Eyes—fagots,
> Lips—old scars, or the first red blisters,
> Breath—the last sweet scent of cane,
> And her slim body, white as the ash
> > of black flesh after flame. (27)

One of the most striking stories is "Blood-Burning Moon," with a refrain that seemingly blames the passionate blacks for the savage deaths of two men—one white, one black—who compete for Louisa's love: "Red nigger moon. Sinner / Blood-burning moon. Sinner" (29). In the blood-drenched canefield, lit by the fire of the cane as it boils away into sugar, suffusing the air and the country with its oppressively sweet, inescapable smell, Toomer's stark tragedy is enacted. The relentless narrative comes full circle as it ends in another fire when the mob burns alive the victorious black lover.

The second part of *Cane* changes location, and intensity, as the speaker comes farther north, apparently to Washington, D.C. "Avey" and Dorris from "Theater" are urban black women, more inclined to carve something for themselves out of life but still the victims of male attention because of their beauty. Some surreal touches heighten the texture of this section, but rather than passion, the northern experience remains one of frustration. Dan cannot even talk with Muriel ("Box Seat"), while Paul brags to a doorman about his conquest of the beautiful white girl Bona, only to find that she has left him ("Bona and Paul"). Unfulfilled people, their lives complicated by their recognition of racism, appear in nearly every selection, and more often than not, these are unfulfilled men. The robot-like "Rhobert," the distant John, the possessive Dan all prepared the reader for the strange characters of the third section of *Cane*, the dramalike narrative of "Kabnis."

The inexplicable Ralph Kabnis bears some similarity to Toomer. At least he also has gone to Georgia from the North in order to teach there. But he is so frightened and indecisive that his adventures in the small, conservative, and prejudiced town succeed only in bewildering the reader. This is no hero, by any definition, and the relentless boredom—of Kabnis's life and of Toomer's presentation of it—is unrelieved by any other interesting characters. Elements of religion are mixed with sexuality that symptomizes only physical relief, not emotion, but the narrative provides few clues for interpretation. Lewis D. Moore suggests that the structure of *Cane* serves to replace the black woman—and her usually healthy sexuality—with an ineffectual black male. By that structure, Toomer emphasizes the negative view of any black man's prospects, "a negativism so complete that one can possibly assume that an upward curve is inevitable if the black man will only learn the lesson of his experience, his now complete isolation from any succor but himself." In Moore's view, Kabnis, who was introduced at the beginning of his narrative as an artist, has long since abandoned that claim, and in that abandonment lies his real failure and despair.[14] For other readers, however, Kabnis is a positive figure because the narrative ends with his ascent from the basement hovel, moving into a day that might see his taking action to go North. Truly modernist in its openness, the Kabnis section of *Cane* proves to be more than usually troubling for readers.

As the first prominent text of the Harlem Renaissance, following by one year Claude McKay's poem collection, *Harlem Shadows*, *Cane* was already known among white readers. Separate sections of the book had been published earlier in the black periodicals, the *Crisis*, the *Liberator,* and *Opportunity,* and other of Toomer's poems and stories had appeared in the vanguard magazines of the modernists: the *Double Dealer, Broom, S₄N, Little Review, Nomad* and others. *Cane* was problematic to white readers as well as black because Toomer's intention seemed unclear. Was he criticizing the naive sensuality of blacks in the South? Was he praising the simplicity of that life, and thereby criticizing the increasing sophistication of younger intellectual blacks? Was he making distinctions between southern blacks and northern, and if so, for what reason? Was he drawing on stereotyped black characters (the sexual woman, the raging man, the tease, the effete and distant intellectual)? Toomer's open and imagistic method, characteristic of the modernist, was different from the methods of earlier black writers, and even from some writers contemporary with him. It was difficult to place him in a tradition of only black writing.

Much black writing during the twentieth century had followed the dictates of W. E. B. Du Bois, who had been editing the *Crisis,* the journal of the National Association for the Advancement of Colored People, since it began in 1910. Du Bois wanted all Negro art to maintain quality rather than be propagandistic, but he also believed that black art should express the best about black life (and he seemed to assume that most art would be created by what he called "the Talented Tenth" of the Negro population). *Opportunity,* primarily a literary journal, was not created until 1923. Until then, black writers who dealt only with the *Crisis* had to be wary of the kinds of subjects they chose to write about and of their treatment of those subjects. It would not do to give white readers the idea that black life was inferior or tawdry or immoral. Through the involvement of Jessie Redmon Fauset as the helpful literary editor of the *Crisis,* that journal became an important component of black literary life, and the two journals taken together were a major force in the Renaissance. Toomer had published in each and had learned from Fauset. But he also had learned from numerous white writers and had been befriended by Hart Crane, Carl Van Vechten, Edna St. Vincent Millay, and others, including Waldo Frank, who wrote the introduction to the 1923 edition of *Cane.* Toomer's allegiance was less to black writing than to good writing, and his politics often seemed at odds with that of the various black movements of the early twentieth century.

It seemed fitting that *Cane* was published by Boni and Liveright, one of the more adventurous younger publishers. They also published the work of Waldo Frank, Eugene O'Neill, Theodore Dreiser, and T. S. Eliot and Ezra Pound (Gorham Munson called Liveright "a representative man of the Twenties . . . a man in tune with the Zeitgeist") and in 1924 they brought out Jessie Redmon Fauset's first novel, *There Is Confusion*.[15] When Langston Hughes returned to America from Paris in that year, he realized that great progress had been made. In addition to Toomer's and Fauset's books appearing from a white publisher, Alfred Knopf had published Walter White's *The Fire in the Flint*, a striking novel of racial violence in the South. Charles S. Johnson, the bright, farsighted editor of *Opportunity*, had given a series of gala literary dinners that brought together wealthy white patrons and publishers with black artists, and led to many new publishing contracts for black writers. In 1925 appeared the collection of work by various blacks known as *The New Negro: An Interpretation.* Edited by Alain Locke, a Howard University professor, the book would become the philosophical cornerstone of the Harlem Renaissance.

In *The New Negro,* Locke and such others as James Weldon Johnson, Arthur Schomburg, J. A. Rogers, Albert C. Barnes, and the poets Hughes, Cullen, and McKay called for commitment to a "new psychology," a new beginning. In some ways reminiscent of Du Bois's aim in his 1903 *The Souls of Black Folk,* this collection, too, stressed the promise of a multitalented race, once it were free of stereotype and preconception. The "new Negro" should not be buried under fadish concepts of sociology, philanthropy, or politics; neither should he or she be confined to images that had existed through history ("old Negro" concepts of servility or rebellion). What would characterize the new Negro would be the spirit of discovery, of pride, of the search for origins—many of them African—that would lend a different tone to art and literature. The situation in the mid-1920s was different; it was, according to Locke, "prophetic." No longer looking to only a "Talented Tenth," Locke called upon what he, unfortunately, termed the "migrating peasant." In short, he believed that all people of the Negro race were making, and could be encouraged to make, contributions. And the coalescence of blacks in Harlem would provide the opportunity "for group expression and self-determination."[16]

One of the reasons circumstances for blacks had changed so radically was that Negroes had been admitted to Harlem as residents early in the twentieth century and that more than 87,000 blacks moved there during the 1920s. For the first time in American history, blacks of upper, middle, and lower classes had created a largely black urban area. In Harlem, the Negro was no longer in the minority; black culture was dominant. F. Scott Fitzgerald's naming this decade "The Jazz Age" underscored the centrality of black music and its importance to cultures both here and abroad. As Carl Van Vechten pointed out, jazz (and other black music) has "an inexorable rhythm"; it combines passion with pleasure. And, further, "Nearly all the dancing now to be seen in our musical shows is of Negro origin [Cake-Walk, the Bunny Hug, the Turkey Trot, the Charleston, the Black Bottom, and the Lindy Hop]."[17] The American—and French—fascination with jazz stemmed partly from its improvisational nature, its spontaneity, its finding form in seemingly random patterns, its sensuality, and its premise that cooperation and good musicianship could lead to art. The antirational approach signaled deeper underlying convictions that emotion was as important as intellect and that an empathetic audience would respond. The immense success of black American dancer and comic Josephine Baker, particularly in Paris, spoke to the immense attraction of the improvisational and the sensual.

In literature, free forms in poetry and less traditional structures in fiction, as illustrated in the writings of both Jean Toomer and Langston Hughes—whose poetry collections *The Weary Blues* and *Fine Clothes to the Jew* were important publications of 1926 and 1927, respectively—paralleled the improvisational forms of black music, and the use of both dialect (the real, the emotionally true) and folk idioms changed literary language. The rationale for the shape of many of Langston Hughes's poems was often the dialect that formed their language (a mother talks to a son, a voice laments its black heritage); speech patterns created meaningful line breaks. In Toomer's *Cane,* similar explanations for the structure of both poetry and fiction existed. Other writers both black and white had allowed dialect to dictate structure. This is not to suggest, however, that black writing in the 1920s was in some way uniform or that all black art was a reflection of jazz.

The music, art, and literature that black writers and artists produced early in the twentieth century echoes that written and painted by whites; innovation and creative impulse were valued more than was conformity to preestablished conventions. Innovation in black art meant coming closer to black language and subject matter and implied a search for black traditions, yet it was not provincial. As Robert Stepto points out, Harlem was less isolated than references to it and its art might suggest. Most blacks did not live permanently in Harlem. They traveled frequently to Paris, as well as to other places in Europe and the United States: "It is hard to confine Renaissance writers to Harlem alone. . . . Harlem was a crossroads, a mecca, but most pilgrims to most meccas travel with round-trip tickets, whether they know it or not. Alain Locke comes to mind here: he was a singular figure of the era, an integral part of what we might call the Harlem event, but he never really left Washington, D.C., or his professorship at Howard University."[18] When many prominent figures of the renaissance are considered—Georgia Douglas Johnson, Zora Neale Hurston, Arna Bontemps, Rudolph Fisher, Wallace Thurman, Gwendolyn Bennett, William Stanley Braithwaite, Anne Spencer, Angelina Grimke, Nella Larsen, Bruce Nugent, Hubert Delany, Clarissa Scott, Dorothy West, Sterling Brown, Toomer, White, and Hughes, Cullen, and McKay—it is clear that Harlem was for many an intermittent location. Part of the problem was that living in New York was expensive, unless a writer or artist found a generous patron (such as Mrs. Osgood Mason, who befriended Hughes and Hurston, among others, but then proved to be restrictive and punitive, cutting off support if their writing did not please her).

The variety inherent in the work of the Harlem writers is clearly illustrated by several texts that were as important in some ways as Toomer's *Cane*. Nella Larsen's *Quicksand* (1928) and *Passing* (1929), published by Knopf, and Jessie Redmon Fauset's *Plum Bun* (1928), her second novel, established a tradition for the black woman writer that continues in some ways today. Both Larsen and Fauset were well-educated women. Fauset can easily be compared with Edith Wharton in that she was born to a wealthy family, hers of Philadelphia, and she also had a fine education; she had graduated Phi Beta Kappa from Cornell and taken an M.A. at the University of Pennsylvania. Later she did more work in French at the Sorbonne. For more than ten years she taught at the highly respected M Street School. In 1919, she became literary editor of the *Crisis*. Her first novel, *There Is Confusion*, was rejected by several publishers in 1923–24 because it spoke about lives of wealthy blacks and therefore did not make use of the major fascination with the Harlem Renaissance (for white readers and publishers), the depiction of "primitive," lower class, and perhaps excitingly different sexual and racial experiences. Like Wharton, Fauset also disguises much of what she is writing about. Irony dominates her novels, but a subtle and understated irony, demanding that readers understand the context of the middle- and upper-class black culture before irony is apparent. The same can be said of Larsen's work; it is much more complex and diffident than it might appear.

Larsen too was an educated woman and, like Fauset, a mulatto. Born in 1893 in Chicago of a Danish mother and a black West Indian father, she grew away from her family when her mother remarried after her father's early death. Her stepfather was white and did not welcome his new stepdaughter. Larsen studied science for a year at Fisk University while married to physicist Elmer Imes, a professor there. She traveled to Denmark in search of "place," auditing classes at the University of Copenhagen. Then she studied nursing at Lincoln Hospital Training School in New York, graduating in 1915 and taking the post as superintendent of nurses at Tuskegee Institute in Alabama, soon moving back to take nursing positions in New York. In 1921 she began work in the children's division of the New York Public Library, where she also began to write. Her 1928 novel *Quicksand* draws on all these experiences, but it also emphasizes the psychological problems of a sensual black woman caught among several restrictive societies—American, Danish, white, black. Its apt title points bitterly to the life Helga Crane, Larsen's black protagonist, faces: to follow her desire for intimacy is to become a sexual object. A definite feminist novel, *Quicksand* shows clearly that, for women, sexuality leads to pregnancy and pregnancy—in most cases—to weary overwork and the possibility of eventual death. *Quicksand* rewrites Stein's "Lena" from *Three Lives* with even greater intensity.

As *Quicksand* opens, Helga Crane "sat in a small oasis in a desert of darkness."[19] A teacher in the prestigious Naxos (anagram for Saxon) school for blacks in the South, she refuses to accept the combination of complacency and inferiority the white southern culture bestowed upon it. In her comfortably decorated room in the school, she thinks quietly of a white minister's words about Naxos Negroes knowing their place in society—and she realizes that she cannot stay on. Although her fiancé, James Vayle, also teaches there, she must leave. Once Helga returns to Chicago, *Quicksand* carries throughout the image of isolation: Helga as a single person faced with formidable opposition, no matter where she is or what she attempts to do.

Helga's isolation is both psychological and gender based. As a woman, she must be wary about friendships, because once her virginity is lost, she will have no value in the marriage market. At Naxos she had to combat the suspicions of Miss MacGooden, the sterile dean who kept her under surveillance; later she had to resist the advances of the Naxos principal, Dr. Anderson. In Chicago, her "Uncle Peter" would no longer help her financially because he had remarried a wife who would not accept Helga's blackness. Taking a part-time job in Chicago led Helga to New York and a friendship with Anna Grey, in whose beautiful home she lived. Luxurious surroundings cannot blunt her isolation, though she feels in Harlem "the magic sense of having come home. . . . Teeming black Harlem had welcomed her and lulled her into something that was, she was certain, peace and contentment" (43). Courted by a number of men, conscious that she is already twenty-four years old, Helga finally rejects the sensual allure of Harlem and accepts an offer to visit her mother's sister in Denmark.

In that country, however, she finds herself an exotic, labeled and dressed as such by her aunt and uncle. Their aim seems to be to use her beauty and rarity to enhance their own social position. The culmination of her time in Denmark comes when she refuses to marry an important painter, a man brought to his proposal only after other unsuccessful attempts to become her lover. Helga's return to America, however, also ends in frustration; despite a number of suitors, Helga loves no one, and she is growing older and more sexually frustrated.

Larsen creates a culminating series of scenes by depicting Helga's sexual feelings—"For days, for weeks, voluptuous visions had haunted her. Desire had burned in her flesh with uncontrollable violence" (109)—and her thoughts of suicide, then having her visit a church and become part of a revival ("saved" as her red dress, a customary color for her but one suggesting harlotry to the church-goers, led them to pray around her), and immediately become involved with "the fattish yellow man . . . the Reverend Mr. Pleasant Green" (115), a southerner far beneath her in education and breeding. From that point in the text to its end, the novel's normal narrative coherence shatters, as if to reflect the precipitous decline in the life Helga leads. She cannot keep up with her work after the first three children arrive, and the structure of the text creates her plight with relentless impact.

Part of Larsen's narrative style is stating ideas in brief, controlled language. About Helga's reaction to living in the small Alabama town with the "rattish" Mr. Green, Larsen says only, "Helga did not hate him, the town, or the people. No. Not for a long time" (118). When Larsen tells the reader about Helga's bondage to the children, she says directly, "The children used her up. There were already three of them, all born within the short space of twenty months. Two great healthy twin boys. . . . And there was a girl, sweet, delicate, and flower-like" (123). Early in Helga's marriage, the thought of the coming night and its sexual agenda gave meaning to her busy days: "And night came at the end of every day. Emotional, palpitating, amorous, all that was living in her sprang like rank weeds at the tingling thought of night, with a vitality so strong that it devoured all shoots of reason" (122). Soon, however, Helga thinks of sex with "a disturbing medley of feelings. Challenge. Anticipation. And a small fear." And after the long convalescence following the excruciating birth of her fourth child, who later dies, Helga withdraws completely: "She knew only that, in the hideous agony that for interminable hours—no, centuries—she had borne, the luster of religion had vanished; that revulsion had come upon her; that she hated this man" (129). Helga's litany of hatred comes to include all the trite religious propaganda the blacks in that small town believed. Without a belief in religion, she was able to see Mr. Green for the narrow and coercive bigot he really was, and accordingly to condemn the institution of marriage. Swearing that she would leave her husband and children, biding time to regain her strength, Helga is finally trapped irrevocably with the beginning of her fifth pregnancy. That is the novel's end, and in Larsen's terse treatment, it is ending enough.

In *Quicksand*, Larsen adapts the quest novel and the bildungsroman to tell a woman's narrative. Helga's efforts to find herself, to enrich her life through new experiences, are doomed because she is caught in a subtext that says only married women are valuable. As long as she is a single woman, she is suspect. Yet she finally admits her sexual feelings and tries to find a legitimate channel for them before they overpower her. What can be more legitimate than marriage to a preacher—and a black man at that? She has toyed with the notion of marrying into the white culture; she has been engaged to a fellow black educator; she has a number of suitors. Ironically, when she returns to the American South, a culture that should represent stability and rootedness, she finds herself used as an animal, a beast of burden and childbearing. In Annis Pratt's terminology, Helga survives only by growing down, not up, as the female bildungsroman creates a very different pattern of coming to maturity than that of the male.[20]

Yet *Quicksand* includes some of the same glamorous elements that made Hemingway's *The Sun Also Rises* so popular. Helga moves with an emancipated crowd, one versed in luxury. In Denmark, "There were, too, those popular afternoon gatherings for the express purpose of drinking coffee together, where between much talk, interesting talk, one sipped the strong and steaming beverage from exquisite cups fashioned of Royal Danish porcelain and partook of an infinite variety of rich cakes and smorrebrod . . . dainty sandwiches of an endless and tempting array" (77). She dresses in outrageous fashions and, if not a flapper, certainly epitomizes the high style available to wealthy modern women: "There were batik dresses in which mingled indigo, orange, green, vermilion, and black; dresses of velvet and chiffon in screaming colors, blood-red, sulphur-yellow, sea-green; and one black and white thing in striking combination. There was a black Manila shawl strewn with great scarlet and lemon flowers, a leopard-skin coat, a glittering opera-cape. There were turban-like hats of metallic silks, feathers and furs, strange jewelry, enameled or set with odd semi-precious stones, a nauseous Eastern perfume, shoes with dangerously high heels" (74). *Quicksand* includes scenes set in Harlem nightspots— "They danced, ambling lazily to a crooning melody, or violently twisting their bodies, like whirling leaves, to a sudden screaming rhythm, or shaking themselves ecstatically to a thumping of unseen tomtoms. . . . The essence of life seemed bodily motion" (59)—and on New York's streets—"For the hundredth time she marveled at the gradations within this oppressed race of hers. A dozen shades slid by. There was sooty black, shiny black, taupe, mahogany, bronze, copper, gold, orange, yellow, peach, ivory, pinky white, pastry white. There was yellow hair, brown hair, black hair; straight hair, straightened hair, curly hair, crinkly hair, woolly hair" (59). For an American reader interested in the modern age, Larsen wrote something for everyone. Ranging from lush description to the bitter introspection of Helga's thoughts, *Quicksand* moves with a succinct—and decidedly modern—pace through a number of years in Helga's life. And for the questioning reader, it provides many insights into the life of the modern woman, white or black.

Larsen's epigraph for *Quicksand* was Langston Hughes's lines about being mulatto: "My old man died in a fine big house. / My ma died in a shack. / I wonder where I'm gonna die, / Being neither white nor black?" It fit better as epigraph for her second novel, *Passing*, the story of two black women who were light skinned enough to pass into white culture whenever they chose. Irene Redfield chose to do so only for fun, sometimes when she was shopping in the city and wanted to eat in an elite restaurant. Her friend Clare Kendry, however, had married a white man who had no idea that she was a Negro—and whose prejudice toward blacks showed in his racist language and sentiments. A double narrative, *Passing* deals with the possibly sexual attraction between the two women (see Deborah McDowell's introduction to the text) but more centrally with the dangers of Clare's passing juxtaposed with her longing for black life.[21] When her husband comes to a black party to find her, and Irene's jealousy of Clare's relationship with her own husband has reached its limits, Irene pushes Clare out an apartment window to her death. While Larsen makes Irene's intention plain, there is enough ambivalence in the text and in the situation to protect her from legal responsibility. Her act stands as a passionate reminder of a woman's effort to protect her life, by saving her husband from another woman, and perhaps as a means of saving herself from what society might see as deviant sexuality. In *Passing* as in *Quicksand*, modern issues of role and sexuality are Larsen's primary concern.

Jessie Fauset's *Plum Bun* also narrates the story of a black woman who is able to pass, faced with the same kinds of decisions about life roles. Should Angela Murray marry? Can she risk the wait into later adulthood as she attempts to find the truly proper man? Fauset's choice of the nursery rhyme, "To Market, to Market / To buy a Plum Bun; / Home again, Home again, / Market is done," as the novel's epigraph, and her first title for the book, which was

Market, makes clear the importance of economic pressures on her protagonist. (Each section of the novel is labeled with phrases from the rhyme, so that Angela Murray's first decision is titled "Home" and a later one "Plum Bun.") After Angela's affair with Roger Fielding, a wealthy white man who has not cared enough to marry her, she changes strategy and admits her love for Anthony Cross, a fellow art student, only to find that Anthony is also passing. The narrative complications in this strand of narrative involve Angela's darker sister, Jinny, and an old beau of hers and are somewhat conventional. The novel is also much longer than either of Larsen's texts, and therefore gives the feeling of a solidly built fiction, one that relies more frequently on careful transitions than on the juxtaposition modernist texts often used. Fauset's work was less apparently modern than Larsen's, but it is every bit as ironic and in its exposition makes a number of piercing statements about race and gender. Fauset also uses an overlay of fairy-tale language and plot, setting up contrasts with the actual happenings in Angela's life, a technique that increases irony.

Although some accounts of the Harlem years give the impression that most black artists and writers were male, such an impression is wrong. Some of the most impressive, and modern, work from this group of writers was done by women, who are perhaps always in closer touch with the realities of daily life because of their roles within the home. But for these particular women writers, in many cases the products of a great deal of formal education and artistic interest, their past experience enabled them to combine some traditional women's themes with a mode of expression that was definitely modern.[22] While the writing of black women during the Harlem Renaissance often focused on women's lives and the problems of self-determination, serious issues for women readers regardless of color, other fiction of this decade was set in a romantic past, drawing on black history and historical figures, or aimed at recreating what might appear to be exciting, even arousing, modern life situations. W. E. B. Du Bois's novels, for example (his 1911 *The Quest of the Silver Fleece* and *Dark Princess*, 1928), tell romantic stories of simple black lovers, rewarded through consummation of their love for lives of frustration and unhappiness. Heavily symbolic (with cotton as the silver fleece that rewards the blacks with prosperity for their good lives, set against the miasma of the swamp, redolent with undisciplined sensuality), Du Bois's fiction drew as well on realism and naturalism of the Frank Norris type.[23] As Bles and Zora work together in the cotton field, they find complete satisfaction. Love is work, and work is love. But the complications of people less idealistic—and less able to work—subvert their love, as well as the plot, and Du Bois falls back on stock conventions to tell his story.

Part of the impetus for Du Bois's 1928 novel was the number of novels supposedly about modern black life, published in the mid-1920s by both white and black writers: Carl Van Vechten's 1926 *Nigger Heaven,* Julia Peterkin's *Black April* in 1927, Rudolph Fisher's *The Walls of Jericho,* Nella Larsen's *Quicksand,* and Claude McKay's *Home to Harlem* in 1928. While Du Bois's comments about Larsen's *Quicksand* were positive, he wrote a scathing review of McKay's novel, objecting to his subject matter of "drunkenness, fighting, lascivious sexual promiscuity and utter absence of restraint." And he accused McKay of catering to "that prurient demand on the part of white folk for a portrayal in Negroes of that utter licentiousness which conventional civilization holds white folk back from enjoying."[24] Because of his strong feelings about appropriate subjects for black fiction, realizing how easy misreading could be for readers who were unfamiliar with the culture, Du Bois in *Dark Princess* chose an international cast of characters. The novel criticizes American culture but provides options to it. In Matthew Towns, Du Bois creates yet another of his idealistic, broadly educated but thwarted heroes finally happy in his marriage to the beautiful Indian princess. In the author's own designation, *Dark Princess* was "a romance" rather than a novel. It seemed a remote fantasy to most readers in 1928.

Langston Hughes, the leading Renaissance poet by the late 1920s, finished his first novel, *Not without Laughter,* in 1929. The book, published by Knopf at Van Vechten's suggestion, began with a Kansas storm reminiscent of that in *The Wizard of Oz* and recounted the daily lives of western black families. The title suggested the philosophy of the blues, a way to meet the foibles of life and survive them; the protagonist was a young Langston Hughes. The impetus for the novel stemmed from Hughes's travels through the South the previous summer with Zora Neale Hurston, in her car, as Hughes learned a great deal about black folk culture, language, and customs from Hurston. Reviewed with praise as the best novel of the Renaissance to date, Hughes's fiction seemed to satisfy everyone except himself. In the struggle to write and rewrite, he had had many arguments with his benefactor, Mrs. Mason, and the final break with her—recounted later in his autobiographical *The Big Sea*—came at the time of the novel's publication in 1930. Disappointed with this work, which had taken most of the past two years, Hughes turned to *Mulatto*, the play that was to absorb much of his energy in the future.

During the late 1920s and 1930s, Arna Bontemps—already known as a poet who had won the *Crisis* poetry prize—wrote a variety of fiction, from the powerful short story "A Summer Tragedy," about the suicide of a black sharecropper couple facing illness and poverty in old age, to *God Sends Sunday* in 1931 and *Black Thunder* in 1936. The latter novel represented a new direction in black fiction, that of historical romance and fiction. Bontemps records that he found a large collection of slave narratives in the Fisk Library and, intrigued by the will to freedom each narrator conveyed—especially moving in the depths of America's depression—Bontemps chose a narrative about Gabriel's insurrection to use as scaffolding for his imaginative retelling of the story. Told by Bontemps's fictional Gabriel, the narrative of the June 1800 Virginia uprising is an effective if impressionistic novel, which makes good use of a rapidly shifting point of view.[25] Bontemps wrote a vivid account of the slave rebellion that—were it not for uncharacteristic torrential rains—might have succeeded. In subject matter, *Black Thunder* was an historical romance, but in form it was as modern as most other fiction of the Harlem Renaissance.

Robert Stepto makes the important point in his 1988 discussion of Afro-American literature that black writers are sometimes criticized for their working in established forms (the sonnet in poetry, for example). Even if critics respect the conviction that accompanies their choices of subjects, they might fault black writers for their lack of innovative techniques. Stepto notes that many black writers may use conventional forms but add inversions (or subversions) to those forms, so that the work reflects a variant pattern: "Of special interest is the play or counterpoint within a given author's writings between 'received' forms (the sonnet at one aesthetic extreme, the ballad at the other) and 'indigenous' forms (blues, folk sermon, etc.)."[26] From Paul Laurence Dunbar and James Weldon Johnson to Langston

Hughes and Zora Neale Hurston through Margaret Walker, Gwendolyn Brooks, Richard Wright, and Ralph Ellison, struggles over
this counterpoint have characterized black writing.

The work of Zora Neale Hurston also illustrates this tradition of
writing in what seems to be an accustomed form, only to vary from
the expected as effective. Trained as an anthropologist under Franz
Boas, Hurston spent much of the late 1920s and early 1930s research-
ing black culture, particularly in the small all-black Florida town of
Eatonville where she was born. She wrote a number of effective
short stories during these years, and some plays, but her first novel,
Jonah's Gourd Vine, did not appear until 1934. In 1935 came her first
collection of folk lore, *Mules and Men,* followed in 1937 by her novel
Their Eyes Were Watching God. Much more than Janie's story to her
friend Pheoby Watson, Hurston's second novel adapted its simple
frame of past-tense telling to incorporate a number of folktales from
black culture. By so doing, Hurston created a mythic, heavily symbolic story that belied its ostensible structure.

Beginning at the end of Janie's three marriages, with her return
to Eatonville after her third husband's death, Hurston's protagonist shares the narrative of her life with her friend. Through
Pheoby, Janie's story will reach the rest of the community: "Ah
don't mean to bother wid tellin' 'em nothin', Pheoby. 'Tain't worth
de trouble. You can tell 'em what Ah say if you wants to. Dat's just
de same as me 'cause mah tongue is in mah friend's mouf."[27] The
connection with the town is important because Janie, at this point
in her life, is moving toward community relationships rather than
the marriages of her earlier history. By serving to bring her back
into a community, Janie's narrative is a kind of confession, although her motive is pride and accomplishment, not guilt or
shame.[28]

Hurston's method of narration—relying on an apparently artless
recreation of idiomatic speech—forces the reader to accept the
voice and language of the black woman storyteller. There is a delib-
erate emphasis on Janie's telling her story in a "womanly" way—
emotional, impulsive, fragmented, intimate—and to a woman.
Hurston's approach allows Janie's story to be truly woman identified and widens the distance between the comparatively conventional narratives of Larsen and Fauset, which were published with
the approval of the powerful male writers of the Harlem Renais-

sance, and her own. Hurston did not want for a minute to be confused with that "Talented Tenth" that was supposedly responsible for the excellence of black art, and her insistence on using as protagonist a poor southern black girl, educated primarily by her grandmother, a former slave, stemmed from that stubborn insistence that the true life of black culture was in its realism—real characters, real situations, real antipathies. For Janie, marriage and its reliance on the control of a black man was the only way out of the poverty she had been born into.

Hurston's changes in point of view and tense fit no prescribed formula. They suggest that readers are at the mercy of a whimsical narrator who makes such changes whenever she wants, yet the truth is that Janie's narrative is immediate and compelling at nearly every turn. Hurston's flexible point of view is achieved partly by maintaining the idiom throughout, even when Joe Starks, Janie's second husband, takes over the narrative. (Joe's incompatibility with Janie accrues partly from his usurping her power as a person. He does not allow her to take part in any community activities, to speak in public gatherings, or to have opinions of her own. If language reveals, and perhaps creates, personality, Janie is bereft. It is therefore ironically suitable that Joe "speaks" this section of Janie's story.) As Hurston moves to restricted third, Janie realizes her lack of freedom, and when she comes into her own storytelling near the end of the novel, that "voice" signals her possession of her self. As incisive as her killing Tea Cake to save herself is her assuming control of her own narrative.

Hurston's language is important because it tells Janie's story but also because, in it, the power of the "folk" comes to life. Not only does much of the action during the community scenes in Eatonville and in the Everglades revolve around telling stories, amusing one's friends, and creating legends, but a great concern with orality had fueled black writers' arguments throughout the twentieth century. Oral, not written, speech had been the mainstay of the black culture. The argument in the twentieth century was whether to abandon that orality in its written form or to duplicate narratives by white writers. Camps were bitterly divided, and anthologies were composed of black work that either testified to the importance of writing in black dialect or of using a language that could have been written by whites as well as blacks. Hurston, by conveying so much of both characterization and plot through black idiomatic language, is casting her allegiance in the ongoing argument with Toomer, Hughes, and Sterling Brown rather than with James Weldon Johnson. When Janie says to Pheoby, then, "Ah been a delegate to de big 'ssociation of life. Yessuh! De Grand Lodge, de big convention of livin' is just where Ah been dis year and a half y'all ain't seen me" (18), she is making a definite political statement.

In addition to phrasing, contractions, and dropped consonants, Hurston relies on maxims from actual speech. "Unless you see de fur, a mink skin ain't no different from a coon hide. . . . We been kissin'-friends for twenty years . . . livin' in de white folks backyard." She relies heavily on metaphor, as in using the blossoming pear tree to represent Janie's budding sexuality as a teenager (and throughout the book). One of the oldest symbols for lust and sexuality in Western literature, the pear tree suggests Hurston's ability to draw from different kinds of knowledge to enrich Janie's story. More ethnic is the series of stories about Matt Bonner's yellow mule, representative of the many animal tales from African lore (and a character as well in *Mule Bone,* the play Hurston and Langston Hughes wrote together, as the mule of Matthew Brazzle, who still buys side meat by the slice to prove his cheapness). After the yellow mule's death, scenes with the waiting buzzards are further illustration of the efficacy of the animal folktale, and the reader learns a great deal about Joe Starks from listening to the words of the Parson, the ruler buzzard. *Their Eyes Were Watching God* also includes a root doctor, a hurricane (drawn, one supposes, from the quantity of black hurricane lore, like apocalypse and flood tales, intensified after the 1928 hurricane still in memory), the rabid dog as devil, and a number of more overtly mythic elements. Yet as Hurston weaves these materials into the text, readers assimilate them easily because Janie's story remains dominant.

Many parts of Janie's story also remain comic. Through intentionally comic language and situations, Hurston draws her reader into and along what might have been a somber and relentless account of Janie's search for maturity and freedom. As Hurston has created her female protagonist, Janie succeeds, and her novel is truly comic, not tragic. She has learned about life through her three marriages, but rather than being a dependent woman, she is able to exist alone at the end of the novel. She comes to know herself and what she can accomplish, and metaphorically she is able to grow up and stand tall and straight (hence, the comparisons with trees throughout the text). Unlike Pratt's paradigm of women's maturing by growing down, Janie's maturity changes her and shows that her culture's expectations—of failure for women—are wrong.

For that reason, Janie's community is suspicious of her, and Pheoby's reaction to her story is one of near disbelief. Pheoby's exclamation at the end of her tale also stresses the metaphor of growth: "Lawd! . . . Ah done growed ten feet higher from jus' listenin' tuh you, Janie. Ah ain't satisfied wid mahself no mo'. Ah means tuh make Sam take me fishin' wid him after this. Nobody better not criticize yuh in mah hearin' " (284). At the end of her story, Janie has become a traditional hero. Taking on herself the double role of protector and initiate, Pheoby serves to prove that Janie Woods (a veritable bevy of trees) has come to fruition, has found her horizon, and has achieved peace. In the course of her journey, she has also found the silver fleece of W.E.B. Du Bois's cotton field, the spacious vision so different from the limited and inward-turning view in Toomer's *Cane* and the horizon image of Frederick Douglass's narrative. More than simply Janie's story, *Their Eyes Were Watching God* is also a literary tour de force, and the reader's recognition of that fact does not detract from the book's effect. It rather allows it a central place in modernism.

6

Modernism during the 1930s

A great deal of modernist writing during the 1920s privileged craft and innovation. Yet even within that formalist emphasis on the way literature was written was an equally strong concern with subject matter. Modernist writers wanted to present the real America— complete with its postwar disappointment and resulting disaffiliation. This preponderance of the waste land theme gave modern writing its reputation for being serious and, at times, unpleasant.

Modernist literature included as well a number of treatments of the by-now traditional American literary theme, the search for self. Identity—defined, circumscribed, and changed by the process of living in America—was as important to modernist writers as it had been to writers of the nineteenth century. In modernist fiction, too, male identity was of greater interest than female; accordingly, the search for self was often made in the wilderness or at sea, environments isolated from peers or family. So long as men were the subjects of novels, setting could be nearly anywhere. Once women's lives became the chief interest, fiction would have to focus on home and family. Whether because the times seemed hostile or because characters—primarily male—were in search of self rather than relationship, most modernist fiction did not emphasize community. Literature of the 1930s changed that pattern because striking changes in belief brought the search for self closer to the search for community. In fact, a character's relationships became one means of understanding the self.

Currents of change were evident well before the 1930s. When Sacco and Vanzetti were executed in 1927, such writers as John Dos Passos, Edna St. Vincent Millay, Michael Gold, Edmund Wilson, and others were bitterly dismayed. Postwar America had been the scene of a number of repressive, antiliberal events—the Espionage Act in 1917, the Sedition Act in 1918, *Schenck v. United States* and *Abrams v. United States* in 1919, increased membership in the Ku Klux Klan, the Eighteenth Amendment in 1920, the Scopes trial in

1925 and the frightening labor strikes, especially the Gastonia, North Carolina, cotton mill strike in 1929. As American attitudes became increasingly restrictive, whether in fear of communism (this was the age of the Red Scare) or in support of isolationism, the country dedicated itself to legislating morals. These restrictive attitudes seemed to be approved by whatever powers governed prosperity because the American economy was burgeoning. The country interpreted its financial prosperity as a sign that its political and social attitudes were correct.

Then came the October 1929 stock market crash, the beginning of the devastating Great Depression. As the country suffered through years of chaotic and relentless poverty, writers came to understand that fiction about the search for self might be less interesting for readers than considerations of the health of a people collectively. Even without a commitment to socialism or communism, many writers began to sense that such techniques as fragmentation, dissociation, and highly symbolic images, which had been effective just a few short years before, were less so in the 1930s. As Stephen Spender said then, "In a crisis of a whole society every work takes on a political look in either being symptomatic of that crisis (which is itself, of course, political) or in avoiding it."[1]

The contrast between the 1920s, the period of high modernism, and the 1930s, an age that demanded anything except that self-involved art, was striking—and gave some readers cause to think that modernism was over. Even in literature that seemed to exist primarily to express the political sentiments of the 1930s, however, many techniques stemmed from modernism. Writers saw no discrepancy in continuing to use methods they felt were effective, even if their themes had changed. John Dos Passos's *The 42nd Parallel*, for example, reflected the new temper brilliantly. Published in 1930, his epic of diverse American lives touched on many scenes and issues that comprised readers' daily lives: the way a person makes a living, romance and friendship, political alliance, the value system at work, as well as newspaper headlines, popular song lyrics, pieces of colorful description of home interiors, clothing, courtship. This first book of what was to become the trilogy *U.S.A.* used more modernist techniques than any other except some of Faulkner's, yet it was considered a classic proletarian novel. When characters expressed the correct political ideologies, readers could evidently understand the most "difficult" modernist literature.

When the three novels (*The 42nd Parallel, 1919,* and *The Big Money*) were published as *U.S.A.* in 1937, Dos Passos added a postscript titled "Vag" for "vagrant." In that coda, the young American man, originally full of promise and hope, waits beside the highway for a lift to a different location, but his outlook now is hopeless: "Head swims, hunger has twisted the belly tight, he has skinned a heel through the torn sock, feet ache in the broken shoes, under the threadbare suit carefully brushed off with the hand, the torn drawers have a crummy feel, the feel of having slept in your clothes."[2] Vag meets only physical insult and attack: "the punch in the jaw, the slam on the head with the nightstick, the wrist grabbed and twisted behind the back, the big knee brought up sharp into the crotch," and stands waiting, "eyes black with want" (554). The contrast Dos Passos creates between the rich air-borne traveler—moneyed, successful, and above all, mobile—and the down-and-out hitchhiker, gave rise to his charge that America had become two nations, a land of the rich and a different land of the poor. The rich have justice, and control it; the poor—like Sacco and Vanzetti—are shut out from the good that America stands for, including that evanescent justice. It was a bitter lament, all the more bitter because Dos Passos had himself been one of the privi-leged, a Harvard graduate who had known the best economic con-ditions and cultural enrichment America and Europe had to offer. He could not reconcile the degradation of people's lives during the poverty of the depression with better conditions that he knew could have been achieved.

Dos Passos's trilogy was particularly strong in showing the disenfranchised poor. The sections of narrative that have to do with Mary French, one of the party workers whose life was devoted to party work, are especially moving. A woman of undeniable integ-rity, Mary yet will lie to her parents to get much-needed money for party efforts, and her intense efforts before the Sacco and Vanzetti executions are a vivid, if fictional, reminder of the frenetic activity of 1927. Much of the protest activity of both the late 1920s and the 1930s was organized, and executed, by women. It might be that women did comprise 40 percent of the Communist party membership in this country by the end of the 1930s. Paul Lauter and Alice Kessler-

Harris point out that much of the Communist party activity dove-tailed with the work of women's rights activists, people who could be persuaded that women's causes were an integral part of all social causes during the depression. As economic realities coerced women out of the work force, they realized how few of their "gains" during the women's movement were real: "There would be no freedom for women at work while millions were unemployed; no genuine part-nership in the home while clothing and food remained luxuries; no equality of opportunity for male and female children who grew up without medical attention or education."[3]

Indicative of the involvement of women workers and women writers was the writing of Mary Heaton Vorse, Fielding Burke (Ol-ive Tilford Dargan), Grace Lumpkin, Dorothy Myra Page, Tillie Lerner (Olsen), Josephine Herbst, and Meridel Le Sueur—women who worked on songs, poems, reportage, news accounts, pam-phlets, and short fiction as well as more sustained pieces of writ-ing. Lauter and Kessler-Harris explain that these women writers worked in a variety of forms: "Each form had both an artistic and political motivation as well as a particular audience."[4] Besides per-fecting the form of their work, women writers of this period also aimed at effective writing, and reaching a wide readership was essential. It might be more accurately stated that the real life con-cerns that prompted writers to work during the 1930s provided them with a somewhat different aesthetic. As Meridel Le Sueur said in her speech to the 1935 American Writers' Congress,

It is from the working class that the use and function of native language is slowly being built. . . . This is the slow beginning of a culture, the slow and wonderful accumulation of an experience that has hitherto been un-spoken, that has been a gigantic movement of labor, the swingdown of the pick, the ax that has hitherto made no sound but is now being heard.[5]

Women, more often than male writers involved with party con-cerns, were likely to be recruited for party writing efforts—and there-fore to have less time to devote to their own serious work. As Debo-rah Rosenfelt points out in her comprehensive essay on Tillie Olsen's career, "The left required great commitments of time and energy for political work, on the whole valuing action over thought, deed over word," even while it privileged literature—and in some cases, party writing was a reader's first exposure to literature.[6]

Women writers were also faced with the problem of having to deny the subjects they wanted to write about because the party assumed that writing about the depression and its results meant writing about labor, the workplace, and the (largely) male psychological problems of unemployment. Although by this time women no longer were employed outside the home because they were the first to go in times of retraction, they were obviously excruciatingly poor. They were faced with the dilemmas of feeding children, as well as the rest of their families; of deciding whether to have children and—as a primary concern—whether to have sex. They had to place priorities on literacy, cleanliness, loyalty, and other less financially mandated concerns. As a rule, it seemed that the party did not want to hear about women's lives and problems or about racial minorities' problems.

Mike Gold's definition of "Proletarian Realism" was very male oriented, focusing on the workplace and stressing the workers' necessary move toward socialism and the classless society. When *Bottom Dogs* by Edward Dahlberg and *Jews without Money* by Michael Gold were published in 1930, the party seemed to have prime examples of proletarian fiction as it was being defined. Both books explored the poverty that was the lot of most recent immigrants and focused more attention on the writing that had already been published during the 1920s by such immigrants as Anzia Yezierska. Although Dahlberg was born in Kansas and Gold in New York (as Irving Granach), both felt disenfranchised in a country that had seemed the apex of promise. Gold, an editor of the *New Masses,* was a Socialist and a Communist, and although Dahlberg was not, he was active in a number of leftist protest movements. As Gold pointed out, a strong link existed between modernist art and political radicalism: "Both were antibourgeois, and therefore antibourgeois modernists ought to be potential allies in the left's cause since their consciousness was so close to that of the political radicals'. Political radicalism offered an end to alienation to intellectuals and artists for whom there was no real audience in bourgeois culture."[7]

Although comparatively few writers did join the Communist party, there was a great deal of leftist sentiment during the 1930s and some overt social action that appeared to be Communist. When Edmund Wilson, Waldo Frank, Langston Hughes, Malcolm Cowley, John Dos Passos, Sherwood Anderson, and forty-five others signed the 1932 "Manifesto," they believed that the revolution was to be not only economic. It also could provide a new and different philosophic and imaginative basis for living—and judging from the plight of many Americans in the 1930s, the country needed drastic changes in beliefs. Irving Howe describes the "genuine idealism" that motivated a great deal of the writing and reportage of the 1930s: "Wilson's gripping report of the Kentucky mining towns, Caldwell's heart-breaking account of the misery he found among southern sharecroppers, Hemingway's description of terrorized veterans in Florida."[8] Writers cared about the Scottsboro boys, eight blacks convicted in 1931 of the rape of two white women and sentenced to death by an Alabama court, but later pardoned, and about the striking coal miners in Harlan County, Kentucky. They were aware that poverty bore no correlation to worth of belief and life-style and that everyone was caught in unpredictable financial chaos. Frustration with the times caused many intellectuals and writers to turn left, however, and as Daniel Aaron recalled, idealistic writers joined the national John Reed Clubs and the Communist-managed League of American Writers, formed in 1935 to create a United Front against fascism. But as Aaron also points out, that united front was split over the Moscow show trials (staged by Stalin to purge his political opposition) and by the Spanish Civil War, which had broken out in 1936 after the forces of General Franco, aided by Mussolini and Hitler, rebelled against the elected Republican government.[9] The 1930s was a period of incredible turmoil, the economic misery evident throughout the country forcing women and men to make philosophical decisions they had formerly never been faced with.

In such an age of change, it was natural that writing would also change, at least in some ways. Maxwell Geismar, writing in his 1960 Preface to *Writers in Crisis,* suggests that "the glittering rebellion of the 'Twenties was based on inadequate human values" and that expatriation was the result of adolescent concerns. What was to begin to matter, once the devastation of the 1930s had set in, was a process of maturation, a regeneration: "The social and cultural crisis of the new decade brought to our writers a set of spiritual positives based, as it were, on the actual collapse of their own society. . . . In crisis the American writer had gained moral stature, a sense of his own cultural connection, a series of new meanings and new values for his work."[10] For Geismar, the shift had been from literature about the individual to that about the community, seeing the individual in relation to the larger whole.

Geismar's interest in the changes between the writing of the two decades is a more sensible approach than the somewhat hasty one of simply writing off literature produced during the 1930s as indefensibly, and narrowly, "political," as has sometimes been the practice.[11] The word *political* today is charged with a number of associations, some reaching back to the 1930s and others newly coined to describe various antiwar and feminist writings. Rather than trying to define the myriad kinds of writing that might be so labeled, Paul A. Lacey makes a distinction between that literature in which politics obscures literary intention and that in which political issues provide a legitimate theme. Lacey wrote recently that "all aspects of human experience can rightly find a place" in literature. "The temporal and eternal questions can have a political content as well as any other kind of content."[12]

A consideration of this problem in terminology is important today because of the unfortunate tendency to negate the accomplishments of writers of the 1930s. A great many writers from this period—among them a number of women and minorities—have suffered oblivion because they were considered political and/or "proletarian": Meridel Le Sueur, Kenneth Fearing, Josephine Herbst, Grace Lumpkin, Dorothy Myra Page, Josephine Johnson, Agnes Smedley, James T. Farrell, Muriel Rukeyser, Fielding Burke, Jack Conroy, Leane Zugsmith, Clifford Odets, Erskine Caldwell, Lillian Hellman, Tillie Olsen, Harriette Arnow, John Howard Lawson, Archibald MacLeish, Nelson Algren, Tess Slesinger, Ruth Suckow, Albert Maltz, Albert Halper, Thomas Bell, Arna Bontemps, and others. (Nathanael West, John Steinbeck, Richard Wright, and Ralph Ellison moved beyond this limiting category—proletarian literature—that might have also been theirs.)

If readers adopt a traditional literary definition of *proletarian,* then such oblivion might seem earned. Joseph Warren Beach, in his classic *American Fiction, 1920–1940,* for example, describes the proletarian novel as dealing primarily "with the life of the working classes or with any social or industrial problem from the point of view of labor." Not only severely limited in subject, Beach's definition also limits the intention of proletarian fiction: "There is likely to be a considerable element of propaganda. . . . And it often happens that the spirit of propaganda does not carry with it the philosophical breadth, the imaginative power, or the mere skill in narrative which are so important for the production of a work of art."[13]

With what seem to be highly subjective criteria for discerning "propaganda" from "a work of art," Beach falls into the trap of establishing specious criteria, circling into a self-satisfaction that Annette Kolodny calls to question in several of her recent influential essays. As she writes, "Since the grounds upon which we assign aesthetic value to texts are never infallible, unchangeable, or universal, we must reexamine not only our aesthetics but, as well, the inherent biases and assumptions informing the critical methods which (in part) shape our aesthetic responses."[14]

If writers were concerned with presenting the social condition, especially the injustice and hardship felt so keenly during the depression, then their methods for achieving such presentation had to be carefully chosen. Modernist aesthetics still dominated literary criticism, and deviating from what the century had decided was good writing could mean disaster. The work of William Carlos Williams provides one kind of example of what could be done successfully without losing one's position in the literary establishment.

From the mid-1920s through the 1930s, William Carlos Williams had been writing the short stories that appeared in the *New Masses* and *Blast* and in his story collections, *The Knife of the Times* in 1932 and *Life along the Passaic River* in 1938. What Williams achieves in his fiction is a blunt portrayal of the poor, the stoic, the actual patients of his New Jersey practice ("Jean Beicke," "The Girl with a Pimply Face," "A Face of Stone"), seen usually through the eyes of the pitying, caring physician. The brusque voice of the doctor, and the economical, almost nonliterary style of the stories, helped to save Williams's work from the charge of sentimentality, though that charge could certainly have been made.

Williams was already a reasonably well-established poet and avant-garde prose writer when he made his turn to obviously political fiction. As he said about the title of his first collection, "The plight of the poor in a rich country, I wrote it down as I saw it. The times—that was the knife that was killing them."[15] Much as he admired Stein, during these years Williams becomes impatient with "Melanctha" and implies that Stein's writing that narrative had been self-indulgent: "For Stein to tell a story of that sort, even with the utmost genius, was not enough *under the conditions in which we live.*"[16] (Williams seems to have forgotten that Stein wrote the novellas in *Three Lives* very early in this century—the book was published in 1909.) According to Williams, the responsibility of the writer in America was to portray "the larger scene." Although he had few models for what he thought fiction should be achieving, Williams spoke with conviction about the stories he was writing:

I lived among these people. I know them and saw the essential qualities (not stereotype), the courage, the humor (an accident), the deformity, the basic tragedy of their lives—and the *importance* of it. You can't write about something unimportant to yourself. I was involved.

That wasn't all. I saw how they were maligned by their institutions of church and state—and "betters." . . . Nobody was writing about them, anywhere, as they ought to be written about. . . . It was my duty to raise the level of consciousness, not to say discussion, of them to a higher level, a higher plane. (*Selected Essays*, 300)

Williams may not have been reading the issues of the *New Masses* and *Blast* in which his work appeared, but there were other fictions that represented the real as well as his, or even better. The reception critics gave his writing, however, was somewhat different from the greeting they gave to writers who began working only during the 1930s.

For women writers particularly, those who came on the literary scene as journalists, their work devoted to describing the poor and unfortunate in untraditional, and sometimes blunt, ways, the literary establishment had little use. Meridel Le Sueur's short fiction, particularly her novella *The Girl*, a composite text that included monologues from various women speakers—real speakers—established her as an important realistic writer. Le Sueur was working in what was a very experimental mode, nonfiction fiction. Yet most of what she accomplished was quickly forgotten.

Le Sueur's writing was meant to erase the line between the writer who was observing the scene and the object of his or her attention. (In even the best work of both Dos Passos and Williams, the reader is conscious that neither man is living the plight of the poor and ill-used character; the writer is clearly an observer, removed from his subject. That distinction disappeared when the reader confronted Le Sueur's work.) "Women on the Breadlines," appearing in *New Masses* in 1932, signaled the beginning of a different mode of presentation, and as the author wrote in a preface to the collection of writings that later included this, "I did not write these stories. I recorded them. They are the words of women who are now dead, lost, incarcerated in prisons or asylums, who have forgotten their names from shock treatments and lobotomies, who went insane from racism and rape, or died from other violences."[17]

Technique reflected this distinctive manner of representation, and Le Sueur's graphic spelling and syntax, and short, blocked-off paragraphs tried to mimic the restrained, plaintive speech of these characters at the point of desperation. "I've lived in cities for months broke, without help, too timid to get in bread lines. I've known many women to live like this until they simply faint on the street from privations, without saying a word to anyone. A woman will shut herself up in a room until it is taken away from her, and eat a cracker a day and be as quiet as a mouse so there are no social statistics concerning her" (141).

She alternates these stark "sayings" with highly metaphoric statements: "Mrs. Grey . . . is a living spokesman for the futility of labor. Her body is a great puckered scar" (142). "We sit in this room like cattle" (137). "We are in a jungle and know it" (141). The rapid shift from character's language to narrator's helps to fuse the narration with the actual scene; what emerges is a total—and totally believable—statement of misery, juxtaposition serving as connection between what is observed and what is lived.

Other writings by Le Sueur deal with women about to be sterilized for having illegitimate children, women institutionalized for mental problems when they are only poor, women who become criminals in their futile search for ways to keep their lovers and homes. *The Girl* (1936) is an unremitting account of a young girl who tries to help her lover through helping in a bank robbery. That the title is generalized only adds to its effect: this is an all too common story, and like Dreiser's *An American Tragedy*, it has no separate distinction of its own. That generality indicts the society more quickly than would a particularized account. Le Sueur's sketches of the older women with whom the girl waits table, the older prostitute who helps her (a pathetic character far from the sentimental whore), and her own conflicting views of her choices have a terrible impact. The reader's admiration for Le Sueur's art in *The Girl* increases upon knowing that many sections of the novella appeared as separate stories in magazines before the whole was assembled. Again, the quick pace of event keeps the text from any sentimental effect, as the author moves from love scene to brutality:

If you didn't ever have to leave here, Butch said, if you never had to go out.

What would we eat? I said.

I'd eat you, Butch said. You're sweet.

It was lovely, the great lovely life he gave me. And then he went to sleep.

The clock outside struck. It struck every quarter hour. I counted them. When it struck four times I had to wake him up. I raised on my elbow and looked at him. I looked at his hands, at his black head, at his sharp face, strong like an ax.

He will be always leaving, getting up from the bed, and going out the door.[18]

Once Butch, her boyfriend, has gone, she has to confront the gangster who has promised her twenty-five dollars for sex. She has accepted thinking that that much money will buy Butch a franchise for a gas station and a chance at normal life.

I said, What about the money. I want it on the line.

Hone laughed, Well she's a good head for business.

What money? Ganz laughed. I got my lawyer here.

The twenty-five you promised me, I said. I hated his cauliflower ears bent on his fat neck where there were sores and scars where the black hairs grew into the flesh.

Twenty-five, Ganz shouted and they both laughed as if it was very funny.

It isn't funny I said, I want it beforehand.

Ganz put his hand on my shoulder. You don't know anything until it happens to you.

When it happens to you then it makes you different and you can't tell anyone about it but you will act different and some day it will all come into you and into others that know the same thing. I thought of Clara and how all those that are covered with filth and are rotting from the same thing will know it together.

I want to go, I said. I don't want to do it.

Here's ten, Ganz said holding up a ten dollar bill above his head, jump for it.

I saw the ten dollars. I reached up and Hone put his hands around my waist. I felt the tears sting in me. Jump for it, Ganz kept laughing and shouting.

I felt like somebody was hitting me on the top of the head with a wallet driving me into the earth, driving me deep down and I would never see anything more but darkness.

Ganz suddenly brought his huge mutilated hand back and struck me full
in the face. I fell down, I thought, forever, into the dark earth. (69–70)

What Le Sueur achieved in her narratives and portraits of
women's lives was a striking fictional accomplishment, creating
moving and powerful accounts of women characters' lives memora-
bly, but literary history views her—when it acknowledges her at
all—as a journalist rather than a novelist. Literary history often
works through very few examples of writing to find its demarca-
tions. If one of our current critical tasks is to trace the shift from the
modernist interest in a character's individual psyche to a concern
with the nature of a community—and with the means of assimilat-
ing the individual into the community—we need to take seriously
Jane Tompkins's admonition to read existing literature seriously.[19]
From that perspective, Le Sueur becomes exemplary, an apt example of a writer who proved through her fiction that life had possibility only through characters' communal sharing—through living arrangements as well as unions. In keeping with the modernists'
aesthetic that form should follow·function, that the style and structure of a work should somehow capture and reinforce its "meaning," Le Sueur's method of writing such vivid prose that a reader
could consider it the actual words of her women characters perfectly illustrated that principle. Perhaps the lives of women characters were less "artistic" and therefore did not qualify as suitable
subjects for writers and literary critics to be concerned about. Perhaps the fact that Le Sueur's characters were poor, uneducated,
and desperate—as well as female, sexually active, and criminal—
added to their unsuitability for literature, but such an objection had
been answered many times earlier in American literature.

Literary criticism is often shaped through a consideration of "major" texts and their authors, though such distinctions are being
questioned in many critical approaches. If readers adopt this traditional view, no modern American author is now more established,
more "major," than William Faulkner. His work, though it remained a continuation of high modernism, did change to meet
readers' insistence during the 1930s that literature change, that it
speak to issues that no one could ignore. When Faulkner published
The Sound and the Fury in 1929, writers everywhere realized that
American modernism had reached maturity. For a novel to surpass

the technical innovation of James Joyce's *Ulysses* meant that American writers had assumed aesthetic leadership. What resulted from the publication of Faulkner's *The Sound and the Fury*, at least among other writers and artists, was the sense that one direction of American modernism had been developed as far as it could be and that subsequent efforts would take new directions.

Faulkner's next book, *As I Lay Dying*, shared many of the same technical effects. Characters were presented without authorial interference, becoming known to the reader through their speech and actions and little else. In his setting up each monologue as if it were being done theatrically, Faulkner broke away from the printed page that looked as if sequential, linear representation reflected life events. Visual signals, then, as well as content showed the reader that this too was another new approach to fiction. Faulkner explained in a 1931 interview, "In the future novel . . . there will be no straight exposition, but instead, objective presentation, by means of soliloquies or speeches of the characters, those of each character printed in a different colored ink. Something of the play technique will thus eliminate much of the author from the story."[20]

While his own interests in writing may have started with his fascination with form, Faulkner was always attuned to his times. He recognized the importance of community interaction and was working toward a comprehensive presentation of themes relevant to its central issues. Thematically, in *As I Lay Dying*, the Bundren family lived their lives within a significant community, whereas in *The Sound and the Fury*, the Compsons had lived much to themselves, conscious of what others in their small Mississippi town thought but—except for Mrs. Compson—not really affected by that thinking. Throughout *As I Lay Dying*, however, voices of other community members—the doctor, the minister, the Tulls—served as chorus to reify the reader's interpretation. Just when the reader had finally decided that Anse was a malingerer, Tull expressed the same sentiment. In this text, these chorus voices replaced authorial direction, a different approach from that of his earlier fiction.

The tendency to see individual characters, as well as families, as part of a larger unit dominated both the structure and theme of his 1932 novel, *Light in August*. Here Faulkner brought together three separate—and seemingly unconnected—narrative lines. The point at which the lines coalesced was the community. Faulkner's structure made his point: people affect other people. Lives are formed through events. In *Light in August,* each character has impact on others. Unlike Quentin Compson, whose suicide in *The Sound and the Fury* affected no one other than his family and the Gibsons, Joe Christmas's life and death had terrific impact. Yet in social terms, Quentin was the oldest son of an important southern family, whose traditional role had been to lead their townspeople (whether in war or peace). Joe Christmas was a nobody, his parentage—and his bloodlines—unknown. The irony Faulkner achieved by making what happened to Joe Christmas crucial to the conscience of the community reinforced the idea that people were interconnected, even if society tried to divide them. The further irony of the reader's being told, in effect, that Joe's father was not a black but rather a Mexican (though that information is also, finally, ambivalent)— while the narrative of his life and death moved as if he were surely black, and therefore outcast—made the social reaction to his killing Joanna Burden even more erroneous.

Light in August gave Faulkner a means of dealing directly with racism. He was able in this text to question prejudice against all people of black origins, regardless of actual skin color. For a 1932 novel written by a white southerner to deal so directly with the issue, what American black writers were also presenting in their novels of passing, was surprising. So too was the vehemence of Faulkner's statement about the mistreatment of blacks—and what the assumption of racial superiority had done to white southern culture. *The Sound and the Fury* had suggested that racism was a powerful issue that, once unleashed, would bring cataclysmic results. Not only is the debilitated Compson family set against the enduring and procreative Gibson family at almost every turn, through the presence of both Dilsey and whichever of her sons or grandsons is caring for Benjy, but there are frequent references in Quentin's section to the Deacon and his survival in Cambridge. The black man, playing on his wily knowledge of white men and their needs, has made being black a way to live profitably. Yet in contrast, Quentin, a white southerner from comparatively elite stock, cannot endure even one year at Harvard and chooses to kill himself from the pressure of maintaining what he sees to be the standards of the Compson family on his slender shoulders. There are many suggestions that Quentin, at least, sees the fragility of his family line and that he marvels at the physical, mental, and emotional strength of the Gibson family. The use Faulkner made of the contrasting white and black families here presages similar patterns in much of his later fiction.

Like much of his later fiction as well, *The Sound and the Fury* is also a novel that questions the power of traditional authority. In placing the family authority in the hands of Jason Compson—alcoholic, educated, and henpecked father—Faulkner undermined the line of ancestry he traced so euphemistically in the Appendix. The implicit structure of the Quentin section is that of a duel between his father and himself, language the weapon rather than arms, and the incredible distance between the two signaled in both their vocabulary and the syntax of their sentences. The heartbreaking dialogue that closes the Quentin section, with Quentin's "temporary" drummed into the reader's mind and consciousness, shows how isolated Quentin is from anyone in his family who could aid him. It also reinforces the impression of the beginning of the section—that Mr. Compson can no longer hear his son's words, and even if he could physically hear them, he is so removed from Quentin's problems, so far past any idealism or romanticism, that he might as well be listening to a foreign language. It might seem too simple to say that Quentin kills himself over a failure of communication, but that is what the structure of his section suggests.

Although Mr. Compson, ironically, becomes a powerless figure in *The Sound and the Fury*, he still is capable of choosing to rescue the baby, Quentin, and of choosing to continue drinking until he dies (he has been warned, says Caddy, that if he does not stop drinking, he will be dead within the year). As Faulkner deals with the troublesome question of who has authority and what the control of power means, he creates the even more despicable Anse Bundren. Anse does not drink. Neither does he make decisions. Worse, Anse never acts at all. The father of the Bundren family has become his family's burden, and his physical disability, his reliance on the heavens (and the neighbors) for help in all parts of his daily life, and his opportunistic clairvoyance (he knows everything about which of his children has money or which can serve him in useful ways) only abet him in manipulating fortune to gain his own ends. That Anse endures is further irony. He lives far past his wife's death, persisting in getting Addie to her family burial grounds, but only for his own purposes. He victoriously completes the tortuous journey, during which his sons' lives have been threatened and at the end of which Darl is committed to an insane asylum—thus abandoning the implicit family charge to keep its members together. Anse's victory, however, is that he has new teeth, and a new wife, and a new phonograph. His children have nothing and in some cases are poorer than they were at the beginning. Cash and Darl are also broken in body and mind.

Authority—especially the ways society confers and withdraws it—comes into question throughout *Light in August*. Because he is minister to the community, Gale Hightower should create the social and moral codes. Yet he falls from grace himself, in his bedevilment over his wife's suicide, and rather than leave the community that is so outraged at his behavior, he remains nominally part of the town. His isolation is so complete, however, that it becomes Byron Bunch's duty to bring him news of the world that had formerly been his. Bunch links the narratives of both Lena Grove and Joe Christmas with that of Hightower, who becomes instrumental in each. He both delivers Lena's baby and provides ineffectual shelter for Joe when he is chased by the crazed mob. Hightower's immersion in these lives brings him back into community and allows him a death with grace: "Then it seems to him that some ultimate dammed flood within him breaks and rushes away. He seems to watch it, feeling himself losing contact with earth, lighter and lighter, emptying, floating. 'I am dying,' he thinks. 'I should pray. I should try to pray.' But he does not. He does not try. . . . The wheel turns on. It spins now, fading, without progress, as though turned by that final flood which had rushed out of him, leaving his body empty and lighter than a forgotten leaf and even more trivial than flotsam lying spent and still upon the window ledge which has no solidity beneath hands that have no weight; so that it can be now Now."[21] In what Faulkner shows to be his final understanding, Hightower relinquishes whatever comfort religion night have provided, secure in his own sense of his personal value.

Light in August is Faulkner's first novel to emphasize community and its importance to individual lives, another stage in his writing about commitment. *Light in August* also introduces issues that come to dominate his later fiction, issues concerning race and social attitudes toward it, and especially miscegenation. The horrifying prospect of the possibility of interracial marriage motivates the community to sanction Joe Christmas's chase and execution. The white community, symbolized by Percy Grimm, carries its anger as far as human expression will allow in its desecration of Joe's body. In this novel, however, ironically, there has been no marriage, and we as readers feel confident that Joe Christmas has a Mexican, not a black, father. Faulkner also gives us Joanna Burden's expression of sexuality, suggesting that she has initiated the affair with Joe as much as he has pursued it. Once again, Faulkner chooses a theme and treats it ironically: the supposed theme, miscegenation, does not in fact exist in *Light in August*.

Joe Christmas is a pale villain beside Euphues Hines. In the guise of the loving and benevolent grandfather (and father, who allows his daughter to die in childbirth, guarding the door with his gun so that his wife cannot call a physician to help her in the difficult delivery), he takes his only grandchild to an orphanage. There he works as janitor for enough years to plant suspicion in the other children. His focused attention on Joe makes him different, and for a group of ill-educated southern white children, being different suggests blackness. Through these years, he keeps all knowledge of her grandchild from his wife. He has killed her daughter and stolen her grandchild, yet she persists in caring for him. The ending scenes of the novel show the macabre pair: the dirty, crazed Euphues—a sometime minister—muttering "Bitchery and abomination!" as he attempts to lynch his grandson, and the wooden-faced grandmother, pathetically eager to see the grandchild she thought was long dead.

Faulkner's most severe censure is reserved for the town. In spawning characters such as Percy Grimm, it allows degradation and terror to exist. It laps up rumors about race and sex, seizes on Joanna's beheading to have a grotesque holiday, and urges its misfits into self-defeating acts. So long as the culture is dominated by religion (religion used as a weapon to force people into channels approved by the narrow and restrictive minds that govern its formal belief systems), its worst travesties occur in the hands of the clergy. The issues of authority and power, illustrated in the white supremacy of the Ku Klux Klan and the military, coalesce in the scenes of Percy Grimm castrating Joe Christmas (who might well have been saved in any court except a southern one if he had had a good lawyer. His killing Joanna Burden could have been seen as a simple act of self-defense—but then his execution occurred not because he had killed Joanna but because he had slept with her).

Community as coercive and narrow—this is the image of village that causes people to leave—but Faulkner juxtaposes positive images to the negative. As people befriend Lena, she becomes one norm for community living. As natural as the trees her name suggests, Lena Grove shares some similarities with Stein's "Lena" from *Three Lives*. Dependent, poor, yet self-sufficient and self-directed, Lena Grove moves through life receptive to help but not begging for it. In tune with other people, she realizes that her predictable life will continue, just as community and religion do. *Light in August* begins and ends with Lena's narrative, but Faulkner creates ironic distance at the close by having the furniture peddlar misinterpret her story. That feint in tone does not lessen the positive resolution; it only protects Faulkner from the charge of sentimentality. *Light in August* maintains its good humor from the happy resolutions for its characters, not from jokes or ridicule about their circumstances. As a novel of 1932, it is not so far removed from the writing of the admittedly proletarian novelists as some critics would have readers believe.

Absalom, Absalom! the novel Faulkner wrote through nearly three years of personal hardship and trauma and published in 1936, also explores the importance of community values. In destroying his relationship with the community, the great Thomas Sutpen sets himself up for an inevitable fall. He will not become a part of the town but will use its values as stepping-stones for his own ascent. He marries Ellen Coldfield not because her family is wealthy but because her family is good and upright. He uses their respectability to disguise his own machinations, his demonic plans for superiority. His rabid design—to create an estate and to produce the best possible descendants to inherit it—fails because he does not value human worth any more than he values community. When he abandons his first wife because she has been said to have black blood, he also abandons their child. Sutpen's pride keeps him from recognizing that son, Charles Bon, even when such recognition might have kept the man alive. The two children he fathers with Ellen, raised to be as demonic as he is, are tainted not with black blood but with cynicism. Yet they survive his warping because they are protected by those vestiges of the community that affect their lives: their relationships with the Coldfield family, with the town, with Clytie their half-sister who cares for them once she grows older. (Sutpen's children by women other than his wife, Ellen, seem not to affect his design, whether they are part black or, in the later case of Milly Jones, part poor white.)

Sutpen is the authority for his family. His maniacal power is Godlike (as the *"Be Sutpen's Hundred"* command suggests). He will share that authority with no one, and Ellen dies a broken woman, a butterfly who lives only in fantasy. Once her illusions are shattered, on the Christmas Eve on which her son Henry confronts Sutpen, she goes to her room to die. Although she closes her eyes to much that Sutpen does, she cannot escape knowledge of his evil, the same knowledge that drives her father to his attic hideaway for his remaining years. Sutpen's voracious immorality cripples everything it touches. His becomes the spectre of southern plantation (slave owner) success.

Sutpen does not live to tell his own story, and in telling his narrative, Faulkner demolishes the autocrat's power. Relying on the imagistic method, Faulkner gives the reader the picture of the young boy Sutpen being turned away from the front door of a southern mansion by a black slave. As he is sent to the back door— no matter that he is himself a white, the black has the power to reject him—Sutpen vows to become important, and he translates that vow into his desperately won material prosperity. Like Gatsby as he transforms himself from a poor child into a wealthy man, Sutpen gives up every consideration in life except that of creating and implementing his design. Like Fitzgerald, Faulkner shows that such relentless ambition is despicable.

Faulkner shows his readers the futility of ruthless power and ambition partly through the narrative design of the Sutpen story. The four narrators who create the fiction are themselves caught in the authority-power conundrum. Rosa Coldfield, as the preyed-upon sister-in-law, rejected Sutpen after he wanted her to have his child and then marry—provided the child was male. Her rage at his treatment makes her act to tell her/his story, but that rage against authority stemmed initially from her powerless relationship with her father. Smug and insensitive, finally mad, Coldfield lives up to his name as he lives only for himself and his ridiculous code of honor. Like Sutpen, Coldfield too defines community as the group of people he must impress with his monomaniacal success (his is moral success, while Sutpen's is financial). In *Absalom, Absalom!* male characters use community, while women characters attempt to work to achieve bonding. Theirs is the definition of community Faulkner privileges.

For Goodhue Coldfield, ironically, withdrawal from community is his most decisive act. He leaves his young daughter alone in the house and store, in the midst of the war and the even more danger-ous reconstruction period, while he nails himself into the attic, assuming that the young Rosa will manage to find food, prepare it, and feed him. This she does for three years. Before his voluntary incarceration, Coldfield has treated her with great contempt, given her no money, and forced her to steal when she wanted to make some trousseau gifts for Judith. But in the telling of her story, Rosa assumes the power she has never before had. Even her asking to talk with Quentin, the motivation for the beginning of the narra-tive, is a powerful act—decisive, cogent, and timely (she dies a few months after she has shared the story with him, in the act of saving Henry Sutpen from the family mansion and its history).

To choose Quentin Compson as the recipient of her story might be a less wise move than Rosa thought, but as Mr. Compson pointed out, she needed someone strong enough to take her to Sutpen's Hundred and cope with what she would find there. Quen-tin does acquire authority in the process of creating the narrative, enough authority, in fact, to challenge his father's version of the story, as comments during Quentin's dialogue with Shreve about the accuracy of Mr. Compson's view suggest. One of Faulkner's motives for having multiple narrators is to allow the duel (begun in *The Sound and the Fury*) between Quentin and his father to continue and to show that in Quentin's passionate involvement with the Henry-Charles narrative, he comes closer to truth more often than did his logical, rational father.

Father-son relationship is a major theme in many of Faulkner's fictions, culminating in the important novels *Intruder in the Dust* (1948) and *The Reivers* (1962). The theme of the father's recognizing the son (or, in Quentin's case, the son's abilities) is the theme of *Absalom, Absalom!* For Charles Bon, recognition by Sutpen is the reason he comes to Sutpen's Hundred. His love for Judith is only a shadowy afterthought. As if to keep in perspective the literary tendency to think all action stems from romantic love relationships, Faulkner shows clearly Charles's yearning for some sign from the demonic Sutpen; and in Quentin's and Shreve's account, his insis-tence on marrying Judith becomes his attempt to force that recogni-tion. To make Charles Bon and Henry Sutpen plausible characters, and their own love for each other more than a forced march away from the Sutpen dynasty, Faulkner needs narrators who are themselves young men, caught in their own family conflicts and incipient love affairs. He accordingly settles on a paired narrative, told by both Quentin and Shreve McCannon.

Resurrecting Shreve from the Harvard year of Quentin's life in *The Sound and the Fury*, Faulkner develops a northern (Canadian) viewpoint to contrast and counterpoint the southern views that mark the stories of the other three narrators. Playing devil's advocate as often as he pretends obtuseness, Shreve holds powerful cards in sorting through the Sutpen story. He is also able, as he listens to Quentin, to point out where his friend might be wrong, where his views as southerner might be at odds with the facts of the Sutpen legend. And it is Shreve who cares so much about Quentin that he is able to ask, finally, "Why do you hate the South?" That key question suggests explanations for both Quentin's torment, and Sutpen's, and reminds the reader that the power of community, and of place, remains indelible.

What Faulkner achieves in *Absalom, Absalom!* is a tapestry of everything a reader of fiction should "know"—the ostensible events of Sutpen's life and dynasty, which is one subject of the story—juxtaposed and counterpointed with everything the culture "knows" about the Sutpen legend. In the interface between the narratives, the reader can find what passes for the truth, so long as he or she remembers that the final truth lies in the hands, and the cunning, of the author, not within the subject. By making the choices he does about the way to tell the Sutpen story, Faulkner has created a monumental account of the powerful and the powerless (Sutpen and his wives and children, as well as Mr. Coldfield and Rosa, Mr. Compson and Quentin, and Wash Jones and the granddaughter and great-granddaughter he murders). Faulkner has shown his readers how easily authority can be abused, by all four of these patriarchs. He has lamented the carnage that occurs when people act on erroneous assumptions, whether they are information based or culturally defined (why does Henry kill Bon, if he does? Because he does not want Judith marrying a black, because he loves Judith himself, because he finds Bon objectionable for other reasons, and so on). And he has shown the wasted lives that result from the stranglehold of both community and paternalistic values, held so strongly that they allow no room for change as years—and circumstances—pass. Again, this novel also bears reading in its context of the troubled mid-1930s and its working title, *The Dark House*, some reflection of the fall of America, as well as the fall of the patriarchal Sutpen dynasty.

In all this labyrinth of story, Faulkner uses as his iconographic figures—those that stay the same throughout—Judith and Clytie. Seemingly the least powerful people within the tapestry, the light and dark sisters of the Sutpen family provide what stability and love exist within the family structure. In their relationship, racial differences disappear, and in their utter poverty, they also reflect some of the issues of the 1930s. In keeping with Faulkner's belief that women are often stronger than men, more self-directed and more capable of sacrifice, he has Mr. Compson say to Quentin, with a conviction that his customary cynicism cannot diminish, women "have a courage and fortitude in the face of pain and annihilation which would make the most spartan man resemble a puling boy."[22] Despite her own bereavement, Judith cares for the other members of her family after Bon's murder, does hard labor in the fields and house after the war's destruction, takes charge of Bon's child by his former marriage, and purchases gravestones with the money left from the sale of Sutpen's store. Her story is one of selfless endurance and nobility. And Clytie's self-abnegation extends to choosing her own death, as well as the destruction of the house itself, to protect the Sutpen name rather than have people discover the travesty the Sutpen family has become.

Once Faulkner finished *Absalom, Absalom!* he continued these themes throughout his remaining novels. This 1936 text accordingly became a touchstone for his later work, providing for it the themes of power and its misuse, family loyalty and disloyalty, racism, community, and gender division. It remained for his 1942 *Go Down, Moses* to express most fully his concerns about the blindness of racial pride, but the rest of Faulkner's writing continued to explore the cost of the individual who is alienated from the community that he had valorized during the 1930s.

John Steinbeck's *The Grapes of Wrath* (1939) is another study of power and powerlessness, with a more apparent subtext about the failures of capitalism. In his narrative about the Oakies' displacement to California after the tragedy of the Dust Bowl in 1935 and 1936, Steinbeck chooses techniques from modernist writing to highlight the contrasts between what Dos Passos had called the haves and the have-nots. The alternation of chapters about the Joads and their journey to California in search of work with chapters about the society generalized in juxtaposition in a reassuring rhythm, rather than at random, which made the text more accessible than some other modernist fiction. Steinbeck's use of the turtle crossing the highway, persevering in its chosen direction against all kinds of odds, is a classic modernist image—as is his use of geraniums, fruit (especially the grapes of the title), and landscape. His title, with all its bitter irony of promise in the American dream now rotted to the wrath of the displaced farmer, parallels the kind of irony Hemingway and Fitzgerald achieved earlier. And his insistence on the real dominance of women—as creators and nurturers of the race—links *The Grapes of Wrath* more closely to much other writing of the 1930s than readers sometimes recognize.

Steinbeck's fiction was political in that it had a clear message about inequities, about hardship among people who had—often through no fault of their own—become the victims of the depression. But it was less political than readers of the time thought because his stand on communism, on unionization, on ways of providing people fair payment for their work was not theoretically based. The controversy about both *The Grapes of Wrath* and Richard Wright's *Native Son*, another novel that appeared to have a Communist bias, seems remote today because readers cannot feel that either of these books advocates communism as a specific political ideology. Both protest the lot of the poor in modern America, and both have valuable corrections and changes to suggest, but each in its own way also criticizes the current state of the Communist party in America. Party readers were not happy with either of them, and although Wright's novel was a Book-of-the-Month selection (the first work by a black writer ever to be available in this way) and Steinbeck's won the Pulitzer Prize for fiction, neither novel became an internationally important text. Neither served to further the cause of the party.

Both *The Grapes of Wrath* and *Native Son* drew from well-established premises about fiction that had been voiced during high modernism. For Wright, his ironic title (how many ways can the word *native* be read?) stressed the disenfranchisement of the black man who had no father, no patriarchy to support him, no house in either the sense of a place to live or a line of descent—

and part of Wright's description of the bleak one-room apartment in which the Thomases try to exist drives home that realization. For a culture interested in Thomas Sutpen's problems in achieving his place in the world, this "Thomas" family had entirely different problems, so real and frightening that most readers would not even try to compare them. The savage blacks who had comprised Sutpen's work force here are the tragic figures of Wright's all-too-American narrative, and in his using violence as a means of having Bigger come to an understanding of himself as an individual (the most basic of American rights, according to our past literature), Wright draws on a complex of both literary and human understandings.

Without seeming to be literary, *Native Son* was exceptionally so. It drew on an earlier factual narrative, much as had Dreiser's *An American Tragedy*. It posed a number of questions about the American family—as had *The Sound and the Fury*—and about "success" in America, as had Fitzgerald's *The Great Gatsby* and Sinclair Lewis's *Babbitt*. It played with the issue of shades of blackness, designating character values in accordance with the color of a character's skin (obviously, through imagery of whiteness in various ways, as well as actual skin color discrimination), as had so many of the Harlem Renaissance works like Nella Larsen's *Passing* and Jessie Fauset's fiction. It featured an ironic emphasis on the role of the young male in American culture (as sexually powerful, that sexual prowess to become financial power). In Bigger Thomas, the reader sees that the size, and the ability to become "bigger" in some phallic sense, means nothing. And with the play on Bigger's name—"Bigger Thomas" echoes clearly "Nigger Tom," with its suggestion of Uncle Tomism, and the original *Uncle Tom's Cabin* (Wright's 1938 book of long stories had been titled *Uncle Tom's Children*). Although Harriet Beecher Stowe's influential novel had made the character of Uncle Tom the image of maternal love, a savior for the racist southern culture, twentieth-century readers tended to see in Tom's death the cop-out of pacifism, and to use the character's name to suggest that ineffectual political strategy. By choosing Bigger's name, Wright sets up the ambivalence that haunts the entire novel.

Native Son is itself filled with ambivalence. It plays with the notion of an outer confidence covering the inner shell of frustration and shame, going back into a great deal of nineteenth-century fiction, both white and black. It scrutinizes the religious dilemma, in giving Bigger nothing to hold to, and therefore despising whatever religious comfort his mother and her peers can find.

But most of all *Native Son* dedicates its energies to devaluing an American belief in honesty and justice, with Wright reacting in much the way Fitzgerald and Hemingway had when they understood the falsity in modern culture. For Bigger Thomas, resident of the Chicago Black Belt, no justice is possible because he is black and his crime involved the death of a white woman. Whether he was guilty, whether he had raped her, was inconsequential; his death was the only payment society wanted. Wright's fiction also shows that his belief in attaining power through bourgeois beliefs in work, honesty, and love has been shattered. Bigger cannot find meaningful work (partly because he was not in a position to have a meaningful education, partly because no "black boy" could be given useful work). He cannot be honest in any part of his life because the excoriating knowledge he would communicate—about the lot of the poor black—would be unwelcome. (Imagine Bigger having such a conversation with Mr. Dalton.) And because no one he comes in contact with has any better life than he does, no reciprocal love is possible. Love in *Native Son* is either a habit or a tool to reinforce personal power.

In both Steinbeck's writing and Wright's, a great many American premises are held up to question. Steinbeck's "answer" is unacceptable to nearly every reader, and for many diverse reasons; sheer optimism cannot solve the myriad social problems that exist in America. The Joad family's retreat to the barn at the start of California's rainy season is only a temporary answer, and Steinbeck's text gives the reader nothing but such temporizing. The literary "progress" of having the Joads leave the dessication of the Dust Bowl (with its echoes of Eliot's *Waste Land*) and end in a deluge of rain, implying that the Fisher King has come, cannot be read in Steinbeck's intention. No reader sees the Joads' condition at the end of *The Grapes of Wrath* as positive. Only a miracle could lighten that bleak horizon.

Just as unacceptable is Wright's resigned account of Bigger's execution. The sheer brutality of Bigger's later existence, capped with his rape and murder of Bessie Mears, cannot be redeemed by asking readers to consider his origins and circumstances. Wright's belief in sociology, in educating readers to understand ghetto life, could not make Bigger a hero. That his life was tragic is not the issue; rather, the ways readers find to identify with tragic heroes come into question. Western literature has few tragic heroes who so bloodily decapitate dead women or so brutally destroy their lovers. Wright's choosing to have Bigger kill two women may have been a grave mistake because the literature of the 1930s had given women characters some prominence. Readers had found a number of admirable poor women characters, and they were critical of authors for whom women were only plot devices. The difference between the way Steinbeck used Ma Joad and other women in *The Grapes of Wrath* and Wright's treatment of the misdirected Mary and the angry Bessie in *Native Son* was wide. The message of much 1930s' fiction was life enhancing and life creating, whereas Wright's novel provided scenes of blatant and mesmerizing destruction.

Bigger's introspective sections usually follow his most heinous acts, as if Wright were giving the reader justification for the killer's motivations. In this respect, *Native Son* works very differently from *The Grapes of Wrath*, where juxtaposition provides the commentary the author thinks necessary. *Native Son* gives the reader first the incredible happening, often in full detail, and then the digression (or the "meaning" of the narrative event). Soon after Mary's death, for example, Bigger remembers with horror "that lingering image of Mary's bloody head lying on those newspapers." The reader could accept his grief over the macabre act, but Bigger as Wright creates him immediately jumps into blaming Mary for his act:

She made me do it! I couldn't help it! She should've known better! She should've left me alone, goddammit! He did not feel sorry for Mary; she was not real to him, not a human being; he had not known her long or well enough for that. He felt that his murder of her was more than amply justified by the fear and shame she had made him feel. It seemed that her actions had evoked fear and shame in him. But when he thought hard about it it seemed impossible that they could have. He really did not know just where that fear and shame had come from; it had just been there, that was all. Each time he had come in contact with her it had risen hot and hard.[23]

The passage does not end there, however, and Wright extends Bigger's net of blame to his whole culture in the subsequent paragraph: "It was not Mary he was reacting to when he felt that fear and shame. Mary had served to set off his emotions, emotions conditioned by many Marys. And now that he had killed Mary he felt a lessening of tension in his muscles; he had shed an invisible burden he had long carried" (109). Wright's repetition of words and phrases, as well as ideas, in this insistent pattern of introspection gave readers to think he was copying naturalistic writing, and perhaps he was borrowing some of those stylistic techniques. But he also knew the power of selection, and he heightens each of Bigger's memories with emphatic repetition. Wright uses the scene of Mary's bloody head to charge the reader visually with the same horror the newspaper accounts in *Native Son* provide for the Chicago (and national) readers. Given human nature, no reader can withstand the evocation of anger and rage that Mary's death provides. Instead of exonerating him, Bigger's very justifications provoke anger, and the trap is sprung even more quickly on the questing black man.

The decade that began with Dos Passos's *42nd Parallel*, Edward Dahlberg's *Bottom Dogs*, and Michael Gold's *Jews without Money* ends with Richard Wright's *Native Son* and John Steinbeck's *The Grapes of Wrath*. Perhaps it would be fair to say that literature had gone in those ten years from lamenting injustice and poverty to demanding change—or at least suggesting ways to create an atmosphere of change. Within those years, American literature and American life had become different—not always embittered but much more tentative. The writing that was to follow would draw from currents of belief, and literature, that might not have been dominant during the 1930s, a decade of surprising—and fulfilling—catholicity.

7

Nightmare Visions

Whether viewed as the ending of the literature of the 1930s or the beginning of the unrelievedly bleak writing about World War II and its decade, James Agee's *Let Us Now Praise Famous Men*, (1941) joins that group of classic American texts that are distinguished for their uniqueness. As Albert Van Nostrand points out in *Everyman His Own Poet*, the greatest American writers are those who attempt to create the unprecedented, as Poe did in *Eureka*, Thoreau in *Walden*, Melville in *Moby Dick*, Whitman in *Leaves of Grass*, and Williams in *Paterson*.[1] Unexpectedly poetic, these texts try to wrench meaning from the concrete, to evoke a kind of mystical understanding from the daily and the minute. In the hot summer of 1936, when Agee, with photographer Walker Evans, traveled to Alabama to live with nearly destitute white sharecropper families, they too joined the ranks of those American artists faced with subjects that had never been 'properly described. The history of American literature and art provided no models.

Walker Evans's photographs are justly famous. The members of the Gudger, Ricketts, and Woods families, the belongings that gave their homes whatever semblance of comfort they had, the stark landscapes that surrounded their meager lives have been indelibly etched on American minds. In some ways, Agee's text is less precise, less memorable. The major change between the writing of modernism during the 1920s and *Let Us Now Praise Famous Men*, though its debt to the work of John Dos Passos in his *U.S.A.* trilogy is obvious, is that Agee as writer leaves the role of observer and becomes participant. One of the most touching scenes in the text is the few hours when he has the Gudger house to himself so that he can scrutinize it in detail: "They are gone. / No one is at home, in all this house, in all this land. It is a long while before their return. I shall move as they would trust me not to, and as I could not, were they here."[2]

Highly sexual, Agee's language as he observes the poverty of the

Gudger household—caught magnificently in a survey of the contents of a drawer—insists on both literal and archetypal meaning. He moves from his guilt at being such an intense observer—"I am being made witness to matters no human being may see. There is a cold beating at my solar plexus" (124)—to memories of himself as child, a boy in "hot early puberty," alone in a house that allowed him sexual, as well as emotional and physical, privacy. When Agee emphasizes his own role in the supposedly objective presentation of the Gudger life, he changes the stance toward reality of American modernist writing.

One of the reasons this change is effective is that the photographs keep the reader at what seems to be a surface level, their power all the stronger for being so distanced. The viewer enters the art with confidence in his or her own ability to read the intent of the photographs. With an aesthetic that has operated in much modernist writing, Agee in his writing also focuses on the stark detail—"A freshly laundered cotton print dress held together high at the throat with a ten-cent brooch" (234)—but he then places that detail in a section that works more subjectively. The detail about Mrs. Gudger's Saturday dress occurs in a section called "Clothing," comprising lists of attire for each family member, by day of the week (the contrast between either Saturday, the day the family goes into town, or Sunday, church day if the family attends, and the weekdays is poignant: much of their clothing is not fit to wear outside the house during the week). The details of this long section become relentless as Agee takes the reader from one person to another, repeating facts in the same quiet voice throughout, but it has moments of comedy. One of these is the section "Overalls ("They are pronounced overhauls"). Agee describes the shape, construction, and purpose of such a garment, the laborer's uniform, with a mock heroic tone that turns to high praise at the ending:

And on this facade, the cloven halls for the legs, the strong-seamed, structured opening for the genitals, the broad horizontal at the waist, the slant thigh pockets, the buttons at the point of each hip and on the breast, the geometric structures of the usages of the simpler trades—the complexed seams of utilitarian pockets which are so brightly picked out against darkness when the seam-threadings, double and triple stitched, are still white, so that a new suit of overalls has among its beauties those of a blueprint; and they are a map of a working man. (240)

Agee's long, incremental sentences suggest both Thomas Wolfe and, more directly, Walt Whitman. The highly effective catalogs of properties and details owe much to Agee's discovery of Whitman's poems, and the care with which he constructs his text—seemingly casual and factual sections juxtaposed with more subjective and intentional ones—is the care of the poet. Agee works hard to make his language have the same impact as Evans's photographs, and he almost succeeds. His language choice is, for the most part, simple and stark, phrased without much formal description:

> the land, in its largeness: stretches: is stretched:
>
> it is stretched like that hollow and quietness of water that is formed
> at the root of a making wave, and it waits: not a leaf, not a grass
> blade, trembles even. (80)

Using verbs and punctuation to create description, Agee's sense of the land comes across vividly, although this is hardly descriptive writing. It is poetry, and that is one of the reasons *Fortune*, which commissioned the essay and photographs, turned down the finished product.

Agee's matrix of language balances between description and interpretation as he takes the reader from articles of clothing to the facts about work or describes in a single paragraph the change in fortune from the Ricketts's "almost prosperous" life to their present existence: "For ten consecutive years now, though they have lived on so little rations money, and have turned nearly all their cottonseed money toward their debts, they have not cleared or had any hope of clearing a cent at the end of the year" (108). His effects are also cumulative. Because the reader knows about such desperate poverty, he or she will take the agony in Agee's text as real. His focus on breakfast at the Gudgers', for example: "And breakfast is too serious a meal for speaking; and it is difficult and revolting to eat heavily before one is awake; but it is necessary" (85). Agee's strategies mimic Pound's insistence on careful selection. What Agee chooses to describe usually carries double and triple import. When he scrutinizes the Gudgers's closet floor, for example, the worn and tawdry shoes he sees there are pathetic in their disrepair and age, but they also are marked with the waste of poor housing and the inevitable filth: "A pair of little-boy's high black button shoes, similarly worn, curled, and scrubbed. One infant's brown sandal. These shoes, particularly those of the children, are somewhat gnawn, and there are rat turds on the floor" (157).

At times, Agee comes close to overt sentiment, as when he calls the wall covered with old calendars and pictures from magazines "a great tragic poem" (157). His direct inclusion of his views about the lives he presents risks making his art objectionable to the modernist reader, but the overall rhythmic structure carries even those very insistent subjective moments.

More often, he lets plain-speaking details carry his opinion. His choice of the porch as setting for most of the action reinforces the poverty, simplicity, and lack of privacy of these people's existences. Sitting together as dark comes, watching cigarettes burn to ash, the family members sense their togetherness as the end of the day's ritual—just as breakfast was that ritual's opening. Being on the porch for these families, however, was less a choice than it was obligatory: space within a house allowed no room for sitting. The fact that the entire family slept in a single room—at times in a single bed—reinforced the importance Agee gave to the details of location.

Agee also includes objectionable details about these people's lives: their feelings of being trapped, their limited sexuality (and the even more limited opportunities for it), their poor educations, their odors, their racism, their unkind competition, their meanness. For women, marriage is an economic necessity. For children, lives are bleak because tired parents often cannot cope with natural energy or rebellion, and education will come into their lives only by chance. For men, life is the relentless grind of hard labor. As sharecroppers, their poor living is assured only during the farming months of the year, yet other work is almost impossible to find. And of that farming, Agee says, "It is simple and terrible work" (306).

Let Us Now Praise Famous Men carries a harshly ironic title. The subjects for Evans's photographs were as often women and children as men, and in no case was any of these people ever famous. Agee's text represents that human situation, however, and makes of it the stuff of art. Through this book, even if names have been changed, the poor white sharecropper families of the South were known and were consequently understood and, perhaps, appreciated. Agee brought into the sharp distancing of objective language, so characteristic of modernism in both the 1920s and the 1930s, his own unfeigned empathy for his subjects, insisting in his portrayals on the uniqueness of their lives and characteristics.

In writing *Let Us Now Praise Famous Men*, Agee created a precursor of the nonfiction novel, the more contemporary text that draws from history (E. L. Doctorow's *Ragtime* or *The Book of Daniel*), autobiography (Sylvia Plath's *The Bell Jar*), biography (Mary McCarthy's *The Group*), or less fictionalized prose forms (*The Autobiography of Malcolm X, In Cold Blood, Why Are We in Vietnam?*). Yet in many ways, *Let Us Now Praise Famous Men* is also a traditional American text, depicting people's relationships with nature and with their livelihood and showing them both individually and with the family units that sustain, as well as destroy, them. Were it not for Agee's attempt to draw the dignity of the pace and tone of the title into the reader's impressions of the lives he describes, the quasi-religious echo might seem pretentious. It does not, and although today's reader might want the word *men* replaced with *people*, Agee does not, in fact, slight the women of the families. He probably treats them more fully, and with greater appreciation, than he does the men. One of the memorable scenes in the clothing section, for example, is Agee's finding Mrs. Gudger's "great-brimmed, triumphal crown," probably her wedding hat, and recreating her at sixteen ("confident enough in her beauty to wear it without fear"), "such a poem no human being shall touch" (259).

Most literature of the early 1940s, however, differed radically from the anguished portrayals of the depressed 1930s, though in many ways this later literature was just as anguished. The major theme—overt and covert—was the agony of war. Whether writers saw its effect as the continued destruction of the community, the theme central to literature of the 1930s, or the reinforcement of the standard liberal view that war epitomized inhumanity in its most reprehensible forms, war was the pervasive subject matter.

Between 1940 and 1945, as might be expected, most war fiction is tightly focused. It is miniaturized. It deals with the lives of only a few soldiers, with the Italian front, with French resistance, with the Germans in Norway, with civilian life in the United States (John Steinbeck's *The Moon Is Down*, Albert Maltz's *The Cross and the Arrow*, Kay Boyle's *Primer for Combat*, John Hersey's *A Bell for*

Adano). The books now considered major World War II fictions did not begin appearing until later in the decade and during the 1950s and the 1960s (Norman Mailer's *The Naked and the Dead* in 1948; Thomas Heggen's *Mr. Roberts* in 1946; Vance Bourjaily's *The End of My Life* and John Horne Burns's *The Gallery* in 1947; James Gould Cozzens's *Guard of Honor* in 1948; John Hawkes's *The Cannibal* in 1949; John Hersey's *The Wall* in 1950; James Jones's *From Here to Eternity* in 1951; Leon Uris's *Battle Cry* in 1953). As Eric Homberger points out, "Combatant-writing generally did not begin to appear in significant quantities until the late 1940s."[3]

What did appear early in the 1940s were novels that tried to compete with the highly successful journalism of Ernie Pyle, John Hersey, Martha Gellhorn, John Gunther, and Richard Tregaskis, whose *Guadalcanal Diary* was a moving, pace-setting work of nonfiction. In the cases of both Hersey and Gellhorn, the materials of their nonfiction often became the stuff of fiction—witness Gellhorn's coverage of the Spanish Civil War transformed into her 1940 novel *A Stricken Field*, or her World War II stories into her 1948 novel, *The Wine of Astonishment*. Because one current of modernist fiction—that influenced heavily by Hemingway's writing—insisted on a seemingly factual, concrete imaging, the shift from nonfiction to fiction went almost unnoticed.

In Gellhorn's *A Stricken Field*, the novel about Mary Douglas, an American journalist in Czechoslovakia during the fall of 1938, the terror of the impending Nazi takeover is conveyed through precise, minutely detailed descriptions of comparatively mundane events. Douglas's friendship for the German refugee Rita is the motivating narrative line, and through this emphasis on noncombatants, Gellhorn draws the sinister milieu of war. Passages such as Rita's trying to escape from Prague reflect that terror:

She pushed on the gate and it did not give. It was made of close-set rods of iron, each rod tipped with a gilded spear-point at the top. Now she realized that she had not planned at all, and if she could not get past this gate, there was no other possible entry. The iron rods were too close together for her to slip through them. . . . She put her hand through the bars and felt for the latch behind the handle. She could not see, so she knelt, close to the gate, to get her eyes on a level with the latch.

Dear God, she said to herself, dear God. It was a very simple bolt; all she had to do was turn the draw bolt and pull it back.[4]

When Gellhorn wrote in a later Afterword to this novel that her aim was to both reveal and record lives in wartime, her statement paralleled other comments she has made about her journalism.

Kay Boyle's fiction about World War II is similar in some ways: deft, effortless prose; a focus on women and families as well as on combatants; reliance on the human detail to convey depth of emotion, particularly of fear or loss. In *Primer for Combat* (1942), *Avalanche* (1944), *A Frenchman Must Die* (1946), and the story "Decision" (published in 1948 as "Passport to Doom"), Boyle uses incantatory rhythms and refrains to underline the impact of her stark narratives:

Our men are on hunger strike! We have brought food to them, food scraped out of a week's or two weeks' ration, bartered for on the black market, a trainload of food, and they cannot open their mouths and eat! . . .

"We must take the food back with us. We cannot leave it here." *The prisoners are on hunger strike,* went the whisper along the walls and through the dust, but the women's mouths were silent. "When Manuel was at Alcala, his wife hardly ate, all those years she hardly ate," said Senora Garcia scarcely aloud, and now something which could not be precisely named had begun shaking like the cold in her flesh. "She brought everything to him," she said, "three times a week, in the afternoons like this—" And *hunger, hunger, hunger,* repeated the hot dry wind as it blew through the women's hair.[5]

Through their subtly indirect narratives, both Boyle and Gellhorn create the unforgettable condition of war.

Harry Brown's 1944 *A Walk in the Sun,* a simple narrative about one platoon during a U.S. retreat in Italy, was incisive and powerful in this same quasi-documentary style. As the platoon marched to the farmhouse they were to hold and then fought to take it from German troops, reader involvement was increasingly high. The novel was about just plain men, apolitical people who were fighting because it was their duty as Americans. Action was paramount, and there was little space for ideology. Eric Homberger points out that few American war novels were antienemy. Fiction of World War II instead tended to discuss war from a philosophical perspective, and the opposition was not between a German and an American but rather between a character with liberal and humane attitudes and one who enjoyed killing—or one (often an officer) who developed a repressive and fascistic attitude during the action. In

Brown's novel, several of the soldiers express their animosity toward officers:

"I wonder who they knocked off," Friedman said. "Too damn far away
to see."
"I hope it's Ward," Rivera said. "Ward gives me a pain in the pratt. All
the sergeants give me a pain in the pratt."[6]

Brown also stresses group identification over the earlier romantic
idealism that marked some novels from World War I. What was
important was less individual prowess, the coming to heroism,
than staying alive and helping other men in the unit. As the acting
sergeant, Tyne, devises a plan to take the farmhouse, his friend
says, "You've cut yourself out a tough job"—to which Tyne replies,
with the cynicism that pervades Brown's novel, "Suicide. . . . I'm a
hero. We're all heroes. This'll mean the Good Conduct Medal."
What happens to the single man is not the issue, nor is a man's
sacrificing himself for the good of everyone else. War is a job,
something that has to be done. When Rivera, the gunner, realizes
what the odds are as the men will walk across the fields to the
farmhouse, he speaks angrily for all the characters: "God damn
it . . . why don't they ever give them a chance? They never get a
chance. We're the dirty god-damned Infantry and they stick us in
everywhere. Jesus, there's a hell of a lot of good men going down
in this war" (149).
    Brown concludes the novel with an almost mystical expression of
this camaraderie. As Tyne leads the patrol toward the occupied
farmhouse, he thinks, "He saw Porter's face, twisted, and Hos-
kins's face, set. He saw Trasker with his jaw gone and McWilliams
with his hands stretched out as though they would protect him
from the plane. It seemed to him that McWilliams had been dead a
very long time. . . . Sometimes Tyne could not distinguish the living from the dead. Faces had a tendency to run together, to blur, to
become indistinct. They ran together like letters of ink in the rain"
(156).
    In the midst of this stark quasi-journalistic fiction, Hemingway's
1940 *For Whom the Bell Tolls* seemed strangely out of place. The very
conventions that he had adopted from earlier war fiction—including
his own *A Farewell to Arms*—had been antedated by the brutal and
large-scale immediacy of World War II. Ironically Brown includes a

bridge blowing in *A Walk in the Sun*, as if in answer to Hemingway's use of the bridge blowing as the means of Robert Jordan's testing himself during the Spanish Civil War; in Brown's novel, the event is minor, and the primary action will not be changed by its outcome.

The image of the bell tolling, the signal of human brotherhood as Hemingway used it in *For Whom the Bell Tolls*, recurs in literature of the 1940s. John Hersey's *A Bell for Adano* relies on the reader's identification with community, and Carlos Bulosan—in his memoir, *America Is in the Heart*—also chooses to conclude with the image of bells ringing as he discovers "with astonishment that the American earth was like a huge heart unfolding warmly to receive me. I felt it spreading through my being, warming me with its glowing reality. It came to me that no man—no one at all—could destroy my faith in America again."[7] Bulosan, a Filipino immigrant, was one of this country's most visible authors during World War II. His *The Voice of Bataan* in 1943, followed the next year by *The Laughter of My Father*, brought him wide recognition. His books sold, though his fame was short-lived, and his photo appeared on the cover of *Time*. One of Bulosan's crusades had been for Filipino migrants to be given U.S. citizenship, and with U.S. entry into the war, and the need for more and more enlisted men, that purpose was achieved.

It is hard to distinguish war fiction from the dark tones of other writing of the 1940s that may not be expressly about World War II. The impact of Albert Camus' *L'Etranger* reinforced readers' sense that modern life had become increasingly inhumane and that the brutality of war was only mirroring many of life's other disappointments. Tonally, there was little relief from the serious. Nelson Algren's *Never Come Morning* and John Steinbeck's *Cannery Row* gave readers characters they had seldom met before in literature, but even these new voices were less hopeful than most readers would have liked; and Saul Bellow's *Dangling Man*, for all its gallows humor, repeated the pervasive themes of alienation and loss. F. Scott Fitzgerald's posthumously published essays, *The Crack-Up* (1945), seemed to be the coda for these war years' angst.

Other books published between 1940 and 1945 were studiedly reflective, not denying all hope but trying to find new answers to eternal questions. Ayn Rand's *The Fountainhead* was widely read, as was James Gould Cozzens's work. Robert Frost turned to old wisdoms in *A Masque of Reason*, as did T. S. Eliot in the complex harmony of his *Four Quartets*. Much other literature—Lillian Hellman's *Watch on the Rhine* and *The Searching Wind*, Gertrude Stein's *Wars I Have Seen*, and Muriel Rukeyser's *Wake Island*, for example—was also drawing, directly or indirectly, on the sobering mood that the threat of death—either physical death or the death of beliefs—provoked. As Eliot wrote in "Burnt Norton":

> Time and the bell have buried the day,
> The black cloud carries the sun away.
> Will the sunflower turn to us, will the clematis
> Stray down, bend to us; tendril and spray
> Clutch and cling?
> Chill
> Fingers of yew be curled
> Down on us?[8]

Some of this remorseless tone of despair was caught in the several books that dealt with racial injustice. William Faulkner's *Go Down, Moses* (1942) was one of his most explicit statements about the waste of human lives, blacks "owned" by whites, even though those very blacks were related to their masters by blood. Indicative of the times, and people's need to escape such harsh realities, the segment of that novel that people read and taught was the partial chapter, "The Bear," the one section safely separate from clear racial issues. In its emphasis on male prowess and the control of property and power, "The Bear" was the kind of reassuring text that shaken readers could enjoy. Its message appeared to be: know your heritage, follow its rituals, test your manhood in accepted ways, and the rewards of peer approval and prosperity will be yours. It is a male prolegomenon; and yet as soon as the women characters in the novel are accorded importance, the meaning of the text as a whole becomes ironic. Once Faulkner had added the fifth section to the story "The Bear," as he did when it became part of the novel, *Go Down, Moses*, the story became a severe indictment of white southern culture.

Lillian Smith's *Strange Fruit* was a more accessible study of black-white love in the South, sharp with warnings of destruction for the culture that ignored human values in delivering its prejudiced, mad justice. Chester Himes's 1945 novel, *If He Hollers Let Him Go*, is the most direct censure of white social forms and attitudes in the decade that bridges Richard Wright's *Native Son* and Ralph Ellison's *Invisible Man*. Himes's book is a carefully controlled fiction, seemingly casual and direct, yet structured to draw a reader into sympathy with the angry, frustrated, and understandably vengeful protagonist. Bob Jones, a young black working in the defense industry in Los Angeles, spends his days worrying about what the whites are about to do to him. Himes details Jones's dreams of anxiety, his rash temper outbursts, his impractical responses to show how unsettled he has become in his comparative success within the labor force. His job has brought him a deferment from the army; and his physical appearance and charm, a well-placed, beautiful fiancée. Yet Alice nags him about getting an education, white coworkers and superiors nag him about being black, and his will to fail leads him to lose job, girl, and deferment in quick succession. Though the book includes a conversation in which characters talk about Richard Wright's *Native Son*, Himes is clearly working with a very different narrative problem: if anything, Bob Jones is too much aware of the dangers inherent in being black in the white culture. Nothing that happens to him is an accident. And because of the objective, terse prose Himes uses, the reader is not meant to sympathize with Jones.

Himes opens the novel with Jones's literal race to the plant, challenged by whites in the fast traffic every morning of his life:

Time and again I cut in front of some fast-moving car, making rubber burn and brakes scream and drivers curse, hoping a paddy would bump my fender so I'd have an excuse to get out and clip him with my tyre iron. My eyes felt red and sticky and my mouth tasted brown. I turned into the tightly patrolled harbour road, doing a defiant fifty. . . .

The parking lot attendant waited until I had finished locking the car, then came over and told me I had to move, I'd parked in the place reserved for company officials. I looked at him with a cold, dead fury, too spent even to hit him. I let my breath out slowly, got back into the car, and moved it.[9]

Himes's chilling portrayal of Jones's "cold, dead fury" permeates the novel and makes all too clear the cultural dilemma of being a minority in the majority culture, regardless of location—Los Angeles, Chicago, New York, the South. Himes's is also a novel of betrayal; the white woman Jones sexually refused gets revenge by accusing him of rape. He escapes lynching or long imprisonment by enlisting, but thereby losing his fiancée and his Los Angeles life. Himes's recreation of Jones's panic throughout the rape charages and jailing is striking. This novel, along with Richard Wright's *Black Boy* (1945), and Ann Petry's memorable *The Street* (1946), form a cluster of nearly overpowering fiction that draws the reader into the center of anger and outrage so that he or she comes to understand the deep frustration of the black characters. In Petry's Lutie Johnson, caught in the cold November wind of her city, the reader finds an image for frustrated self-sacrifice, useless self-sacrifice, that is nearly indelible. The novel is a tone poem of the relentless destruction of Lutie and her young son, Bub, ground under by the community of the street until nothing remains of their promise.

The conviction of these black writers appears also in Gwendolyn Brooks's *A Street in Bronzeville,* a collection of finely crafted poems that had as its theme the waste of human vitality in the black ghetto. The "door-locked dirtiness" of Matthew Cole's rented room, the hunchback girl, Mrs. Martin's Booker T., Satin-Legs Smith: Brooks's places and characters gave further credibility to the poverty and anger Petry, Wright, and Himes drew so vividly. Her comparative pastels echoed, and subtly reinforced, the impact of this prose by black American writers, as in the opening lines of "kitchenette building":

> We are things of dry hours and the involuntary plan,
> Grayed in, and gray. "Dream" makes a giddy sound, not strong
> Like "rent," "feeding a wife," "satisfying a man."[10]

Because "black writing" was considered separate from mainstream writing, the impact that should have been inevitable became scattered, and the general sense of fiction of the 1940s was more conservative and somewhat less interesting than writing produced during earlier decades of modernism.

The early 1940s appeared to be a time of stock-taking, of sorting through values that had come into question during the Great Depression, and of values that had been born of that crisis. But the movement toward community solidarity, the interest in socialism as well as communism, ended abruptly. Nothing remotely connected with fascism could exist in American culture of the 1940s, and the turn to conservatism that peaked with the election of

Dwight D. Eisenhower in 1952 began soon after World War II. Book publishers were affected by the direction of political views as well, and the mediocrity of restatement, the tested and sure repetition of accepted views, comprised much literature published during the 1940s.

There were new, younger writers, searching with the intensity of a youth now scarred by a major war, even if a war geographically remote: Carson McCullers, Truman Capote, Paul Bowles, Robert Lowell, Wright Morris, Saul Bellow, Jean Stafford, Theodore Roethke, Delmore Schwartz. The direction of most of their art was inward, as was the work of many of the writers already established. Only among the black writers (Chester Himes, Richard Wright, Ann Petry, Gwendolyn Brooks, Margaret Walker) was there an insistence on community and caring—expressed negatively in the male writers and more positively in the female. More of the rest of the writing of the early 1940s tended to record and perhaps lament the past (Caroline Gordon's *The Women on the Porch*, John Dos Passos's *Number One*, Tennessee Williams's *The Glass Menagerie*, and much of Eudora Welty's fiction) or to look into the traditions of literature, and of literary practice, for both themes and reassurance.

Literature in the early 1940s was not adventurous, and the crystalline momentum that technical innovation—the sense of the new—had given to modernism was sharply curtailed. As Chester Eisinger concluded, literature of these war years was "inward-turning and backward-turning." In rejecting its own contemporary world, it found temporary calm. In making use of myth as part of literary tradition, such as Welty used in *The Robber Bridegroom*, it traded the modernist sense of making the world anew for the satisfaction of sharing in worlds long established—and perhaps somehow safe from the wholesale destruction of another world war.[11]

In the 1940s, American literature finally shook loose from the hold that modernism had so powerfully established on the minds and craft of its writers and readers. Its loss was hardly noticed—at least not for more than a decade, when the rebellious literati of the 1960s resurrected much of its aesthetic. For the time being, the years of World War II, readers were content to find old worlds, old ideas, and old words, predictable and reassuringly undamaged by what was to be recognized later as one of modern time's great holocausts.

Notes

PREFACE

1. Nina Baym, "Melodramas of Beset Manhood: How Theories of American Fiction Exclude Women Authors," *American Quarterly* 33, no. 2 (Summer 1981):123–49.

2. Annette Kolodny, "Dancing through the Minefield: Some Observations on the Theory, Practice and Politics of a Feminist Literary Criticism," *Feminist Studies* 6, no. 1 (Spring 1980):1–25, and "A Map for Rereading; Or, Gender and the Interpretation of Literary Texts," *New Literary History* 11 (1979–80):451–67.

CHAPTER 1

1. Virginia Woolf, "Mr. Bennett and Mrs. Brown," in *Collected Essays* (London: Hogarth Press, 1966–67), 1:96.

2. Among the good studies of modernism that focus on Bergsonian and other concepts of time are J. P. Hodin, *Modern Art and the Modern Mind* (Cleveland: Press of Case Western Reserve University, 1972); Graham Hough, *Image and Experience: Studies in a Literary Revolution* (London: Duckworth, 1960); Hugh Kenner, *The Pound Era* (Berkeley: University of California Press, 1971); Paul Douglas, *Bergson, Eliot, and American Literature* (Lexington: University of Kentucky Press, 1986).

3. Maurice Beebe, "What Modernism Was," *Journal of Modern Literature* 3, no. 5 (July 1974):1065–84.

4. Gaylord Leroy and Ursula Beitz, "The Marxist Approach to Modernism," *Journal of Modern Literature* 3, no. 5 (July 1974):1158–74.

5. Quentin Anderson, "The Emergence of Modernism," in Emory Elliott, ed., *Columbia Literary History of the United States* (New York: Columbia University Press, 1988), 713.

6. Edmund Wilson, *The Shores of Light* (New York: Farrar, Straus and Young, 1952), 15.

7. Gorham Munson, "A Comedy of Exiles," *Literary Review* 12, no. 1 (Autumn 1968): 47.

8. T. S. Eliot, quoted in *The Literary Essays of Ezra Pound* (Norfolk, Conn.: New Directions, 1935), 114.

9. John Dos Passos, *Occasions and Protests* (New York: Henry Regnery, 1965), 5.

10. John Dos Passos, Foreword to Blaise Cendrars, *Panama, Or, The Adventures of My Seven Uncles* (New York: Harper and Brothers, 1931).

11. T. S. Eliot, recorded comment, in *The Waste Land, A Facsimile and Transcript of the Original Drafts*, ed. Valerie Eliot (New York: Harcourt Brace Jovanovich, 1971), 1. The original epigraph to the poem was from Conrad: "Did he live his life again in every detail of desire, temptation, and surrender during that supreme moment of complete knowledge? He cried in a whisper at some image, at some vision. . . . 'The Horror! the horror!' "

12. Andrew Ross, *The Failure of Modernism: Symptoms of American Poetry* (New York: Columbia University Press, 1986). See also Alan Wilde, *Horizons of Assent, Modernism, Postmodernism, and the Ironic Imagination* (Baltimore: Johns Hopkins University Press, 1981), and Morton P. Levitt, *Modernist Survivors* (Columbus: Ohio State University Press, 1987).

13. Sandra M. Gilbert and Susan Gubar, *No Man's Land: The Place of the Woman Writer in the Twentieth Century* (New Haven, Conn: Yale University Press, 1988), 1:75–76, 99–100.

14. Shari Benstock, *Women of the Left Bank, Paris, 1900–1940* (Austin: University of Texas Press, 1986), 6. See also Cecelia Tichi, "Women Writers and the New Woman" and Elaine Showalter, "Women Writers between the Wars," in Elliott, *Columbia Literary History*, 589–606 and 822–41, respectively.

CHAPTER 2

1. John J. Conder, *Naturalism in American Fiction: The Classic Phase* (Lexington: University Press of Kentucky, 1984); Charles Child Walcutt, *American Literary Naturalism: A Divided Stream* (Minneapolis: University of Minnesota Press, 1956); Nina Baym, "Melodramas of Beset Manhood: How Theories of American Fiction Exclude Women Authors," *American Quarterly* 33, no. 2 (Summer 1981):123–49.

2. Morris Beja, *Epiphany in the Modern Novel* (London: Peter Owen, 1971); Ralph Freedman, *The Lyrical Novel* (Princeton, N.J.: Princeton University Press, 1963).

3. Freedman, *Lyrical Novel*. Also see Henri Bergson, *Time and Free Will: An Essay on the Immediate Data of Consciousness*, trans. F. L. Pogson (London: George Allen and Unwin, 1910).

4. Needed is a study of this period in literature that corresponds with that of Nina Baym in *Novels, Readers, and Reviewers: Responses to Fiction in Antebellum America* (Ithaca, N.Y.: Cornell University Press, 1984).

5. Sandra M. Gilbert and Susan Gubar, *The Madwoman in the Attic: The Woman Writer and the Nineteenth-Century Imagination* (New Haven, Conn.: Yale University Press, 1979).

6. Both Wharton and Glasgow wrote reviews and essays about writing seriously and collected appropriate essays into a book later in their careers. Glasgow was honored by having two series of her novels published as sets, and for the so-called Virginia Edition, she wrote prefaces for each novel, reminiscent of those by Henry James. Her prefaces were published in 1943 as *A Certain Measure: An Interpretation of Prose Fiction*.

7. Mentioned by Scott Donaldson in a 1985 discussion at Key West, Florida.

8. Willa Cather, *My Ántonia* (Boston: Houghton Mifflin, 1918), 370, 321 (hereafter cited parenthetically in the text).

9. Willa Cather, *A Lost Lady* (New York: Vintage 1972), 134 (hereafter cited parenthetically in the text).

10. Willa Cather, *Not Under 40* (New York: Knopf, 1936), 44, 48.

11. Gertrude Stein, *Three Lives* (New York: Vintage, 1909), 11, 24, 80 (hereafter cited parenthetically in the text).

12. Claude McKay, *A Long Way from Home* (New York: Lee Furman, 1937), 248.

13. Sherwood Anderson, *Winesburg, Ohio* (New York: Modern Library, 1947), 184.

14. Gertrude Stein, *Lectures in America* (Boston: Beacon, 1959), 138.

15. Anderson as quoted in Ray Lewis White, "A Critical Analysis," *Readers and Writers* 1, no. 6 (April 1968):36.

16. Sherwood Anderson, "Death in the Woods," in *The Portable Sherwood Anderson*, ed. Horace Gregory (New York: Viking, 1949), 533, 542, 534 (hereafter cited parenthetically in the text).

CHAPTER 3

1. John Dos Passos, *The Best Times* (New York: New American Library, 1966), 24.

2. "A Few Don'ts by an Imagiste," *Poetry* 1, no. 6 (March 1913):200–201.

3. Ezra Pound, "Imagism," *Poetry* 1, no. 6 (March 1913):199. See also Pound's essay "Vorticism," *Fortnightly Review*, 1 September 1914, 469.

4. Pound, "Imagism," 200–201.

5. Jay McCormick, *The Middle Distance: A Comparative History of American Imaginative Literature, 1919–1932* (New York: Free Press, 1971), 88.

6. Judith Sensibar, *The Origins of Faulkner's Art* (Austin: University of Texas Press, 1984), accompanied by the reprinted text, *Vision in Spring* (Austin: University of Texas Press, 1984), an early poem sequence.

7. Joseph Blotner, *Faulkner: A Biography* (New York: Random House, 1974), 452, 47, Notes. For a complete discussion of the milieu in which the modernists matured, see my *Hemingway and Faulkner: inventors/masters* (Metuchen, N.J.: Scarecrow Press, 1975).

8. John Dos Passos, *A Pushcart at the Curb* (New York: Doran & Co., 1977), 43.

9. Quoted by Carlos Baker in *Ernest Hemingway, A Life Story* (New York: Scribner's, 1969), 82.

10. William Faulkner, *The Marble Faun and A Green Bough* (1933; reprint ed., New York: Random House, 1965), 44.

11. Ezra Pound, *Literary Essays of Ezra Pound* (Norfolk, Conn: New Directions, 1935), 50.

12. Ezra Pound, "Small Magazines," *English Journal* 19, no. 9 (November 1930): 700.

13. William J. Handy, *Modern Fiction: A Formalist Approach* (Carbondale: Southern Illinois University Press, 1971), 15ff.

14. Ernest Hemingway, *The Complete Short Stories* (New York: Charles Scribner's Sons, 1987), 79, 288, 161.

15. Ernest Hemingway, *In Our Time* (New York: Scribner's, 1930), (hereafter cited parenthetically in the text).

16. Ernest Hemingway, "A Man's Credo," *Playboy* 10, no. 1 (January 1963).

17. William Faulkner, *Lion in the Garden*, ed. James B. Meriwether and Michael Millgate (New York: Random House, 1968), 55, 32; *Faulkner at West Point*, ed. Joseph L. Fant III and Robert Ashley (New York: Random House, 1964), 73.

18. Faulkner, *Lion in the Garden*, 18.

19. H.D., "Fragment Thirty-Six," in *Chief Modern Poets of England and America*, ed. Gerald Dewitt Sanders, John Herbert Nelson, and M. L. Rosenthal (New York: Macmillan, 1962), 2:211.

20. Carol Gilligan, *In a Different Voice: Psychological Theory and Women's Development* (Cambridge, Mass.: Harvard University Press, 1982), 73, 159ff. Congruent with Gilligan's theories is Rachel Blau DuPlessis's study of narrative, *Writing beyond the Ending: Narrative Strategies of Twentieth-Century Women Writers* (Bloomington: Indiana University Press, 1985), which includes substantial discussion of H.D.'s work.

21. H.D., *HERmione* (New York: New Directions, 1981), 70.

22. John Dos Passos, *The 42nd Parallel* (New York: New American Library, 1930), 101 (hereafter cited parenthetically in the text).

23. T. S. Eliot, Introduction to *Nightwood: The Selected Works of Djuna Barnes* (New York: Farrar, Straus, Cudahy, 1962), 228.

24. Gertrude Stein, *Tender Buttons, Selected Writings of Gertrude Stein*, ed. Carl Van Vechten (New York: Random House, 1962), 464.

25. William Carlos Williams, "The Work of Gertrude Stein," in *Selected Essays of William Carlos Williams* (New York: Random House, 1954), 118.

26. Randa Dubnick, *The Structure of Obscurity: Gertrude Stein, Language, and Cubism* (Urbana: University of Illinois Press, 1984), p. 34.

27. Henri Bergson, *Introduction to Metaphysics*, trans. T. E. Hulme (1912; reprint ed., Indianapolis: Indiana: Liberal Arts Press, 1955), 27–28.

CHAPTER 4

1. Ernest Hemingway, letter dated 18 October 1924, quoted by Edmund Wilson in *The Shores of Light* (New York: Farrar, Straus and Young, 1952), 122.

2. Ellen Glasgow, *Barren Ground* (Garden City, N.Y.: Grosset and Dunlap, 1925), 125 (hereafter cited parenthetically in the text).

3. Edith Wharton, *The Mother's Recompense* (New York: D. Appleton, 1925), 329.

4. Anzia Yezierska, *Bread Givers* (New York: Persea, 1975), 268.

5. John Dos Passos, *Manhattan Transfer* (Boston: Houghton Mifflin, 1925), 3.

6. Sinclair Lewis; *Arrowsmith* (New York: Harcourt, Brace, Jovanovich, 1925), 364–65.

7. Sherwood Anderson, *Dark Laughter* (New York: Liveright, 1925), 183.

8. William Carlos Williams, *In the American Grain* (New York: Albert and Charles Boni, 1925), 183–84.

9. Leon Katz, Introduction to Gertrude Stein, *Fernhurst, Q.E.D., and Other Early Writings* (New York: Liveright, 1971), ix–xlii; see also Donald Gallup's essay, "The Making of *The Making of Americans*."

CHAPTER 5

1. Ernest Hemingway, *A Moveable Feast* (New York: Charles Scribner's Son, 1964), 7.

2. Janis P. Stout, *The Journey Narrative in American Literature: Patterns and Departures* (Westport, Conn.: Greenwood, 1983), 30–31.

3. Malcolm Cowley, *A Second Flowering* (New York: Viking, 1973), 53.

4. Man Ray, quoted by Alfred Kazin in *An American Procession* (New York: Random House, 1984), 380.

5. Benstock, *Women.*

6. Kazin, *American Procession,* p. 380.

7. Gertrude Stein, *The Autobiography of Alice B. Toklas,* in *Selected Writings of Gertrude Stein,* ed. Carl Van Vechten (New York: Vintage, 1962), 6.

8. William Carlos Williams, *The Autobiography of William Carlos Williams* (New York: Random House, 1951), 190.

9. Ernest Hemingway, *The Sun Also Rises* (New York: Charles Scribner's Sons, 1926), 11 (hereafter cited parenthetically in text).

10. Scott Donaldson, "Humor in *The Sun Also Rises*" in *New Essays on The Sun Also Rises,* ed. Linda Wagner-Martin (New York: Cambridge University Press, 1987), p. 37. See also James Hinkle, "What's Funny in *The Sun Also Rises,*" in *Ernest Hemingway, Six Decades of Criticism,* ed. Linda W. Wagner (East Lansing: Michigan State University Press, 1987), 77–92, and Wagner, *Hemingway and Faulkner.*

11. Ernest Hemingway, *in our time* (Paris: Three Mountains Press, 1924), title page epigraph.

12. Quoted in Darwin T. Turner, Introduction to Jean Toomer, *Cane* (New York: Liveright, 1975), xvi.

13. Toomer, *Cane,* 1 (hereafter cited parenthetically in text).

14. Lewis D. Moore, "Kabnis and the Reality of Hope: Jean Toomer's *Cane,*" *North Dakota Quarterly* 54, no. 1 (Winter 1986):37.

15. Gorham Munson, *The Awakening Twenties* (Baton Rouge: Louisiana State University Press, 1985), 137.

16. Material in *The New Negro* was originally published in a special issue of Locke's *Survey Graphic* (Vol. 6, March 1925), and in that collection, Locke published two essays, "Harlem" and "Enter the New Negro."

17. Carl Van Vechten, *The Dance Writings of Carl Van Vechten,* ed. Paul Padgette (New York: Dance Horizons, 1974), 38–39.

18. Robert Stepto, "Afro-American Literature," in Elliott, *Columbia Literary History,* 795.

19. Nella Larsen, *Quicksand,* in *Quicksand and Passing* (New Brunswick,

N.J.: Rutgers University Press, 1986), p. 1 (hereafter cited parenthetically in the text).

20. Annis Pratt, *Archetypal Patterns in Women's Fiction* (Bloomington: Indiana University Press, 1981).

21. McDowell, Introduction to *Quicksand and Passing*, xxvi–xxvii.

22. See *The Harlem Renaissance Re-Examined*, ed. Victor A. Kramer (New York: AMS Press, 1988), especially Nellie Y. McKay's " 'What Were They Saying?' A Selected Overview of Black Women Playwrights of the Harlem Renaissance" and Armitjit Singh's "Black-White Symbiosis: Another Look at the Literary History of the 1920s."

23. Arnold Rampersad, *The Art and Imagination of W.E.B. Du Bois* (Cambridge, Mass.: Harvard University Press, 1976), 117ff.

24. W. E. B. Du Bois, "Two Novels," *Crisis* 35 (June 1928):202.

25. Arna Bontemps, Introduction to *Black Thunder* (Boston: Beacon Press, 1968, rpt. 1936).

26. Stepto, *Columbia* 796–97. See also Robert Hemenway, "The Sacred Canon and Brazzle's Mule, *ADE Bulletin* 73 (Winter 1982):26–32.

27. Zora Neale Hurston, *Their Eyes Were Watching God* (Urbana: University of Illinois Press, 1978), 17 (hereafter cited parenthetically in the text).

28. Terrence Doody, *Confession and Community in the Novel* (Baton Rouge: Louisiana State University Press, 1980), 7–13.

CHAPTER 6

1. Stephen Spender, *The 1930s and After* (New York: Random House, 1978), 13.

2. John Dos Passos, *The Big Money* (New York: New American Library, 1936), 553 (hereafter cited parenthetically in the text).

3. Paul Lauter and Alice Kessler-Harris, Introduction to Fielding Burke, *Call Home the Heart, A Novel of the Thirties* (Old Westbury, N.Y.: Feminist Press, 1983), viii.

4. Ibid., ix.

5. As quoted in ibid., x; also available in *Proceedings of the American Writers' Congress* (Minneapolis: West End Press, 1981).

6. Deborah Rosenfelt, "From the Thirties: Tillie Olsen and the Radical Tradition," in *Feminist Criticism and Social Change*, ed. Judith Newton and Deborah Rosenfelt (New York: Methuen, 1985), 225.

7. Ralph F. Bogardus and Fred Hobson, Introduction to *Literature at the Barricades: The American Writer in the 1930s* (University: University of Alabama Press, 1982), 5. See also Daniel Aaron, *Writers on the Left* (New York: Harcourt, Brace and World, 1961), Walter B. Rideout, *The Radical Novel in the United States, 1900–1954* (Cambridge, Mass.: Harvard University Press, 1956), and *Writing Red: An Anthology of American Women Writers, 1930–1940*, ed. Charlotte Nekola and Paula Rabinowitz (New York: The Feminist Press, 1987).

8. Irving Howe, "The Thirties in Retrospect" in Bogardus and Hobson, *Literature*, 15, 17.

9. Daniel Aaron, "Literary Scenes and Literary Movements," in Elliott, *Columbia Literary History*, 747–49.

10. Maxwell Geismar, *Writers in Crisis, The American Novel, 1925–1940* (New York: E. P. Dutton, 1971), xiii, xv.

11. Recent anthologies of American literature (for example, the Harper) have all but dispensed with writers who dealt with this period or these issues. See Nina Baym's "Melodramas of Beset Manhood: How Theories of American Fiction Exclude Women Authors," *American Quarterly* 33, no. 2 (Summer 1981):123–49, for ideas about the obliteration of books and writers who no longer fit into concepts of appropriate directions for literature.

12. Paul A. Lacey, "The Poetry of Political Anguish," *Sagetrieb* 4, no. 1 (Spring 1985):63.

13. Joseph Warren Beach, *American Fiction, 1920–1940* (New York: Russell & Russell, 1960), 327.

14 Kolodny, "Dancing through the Minefield," 1–25, and "A Map for Rereading: Or, Gender and the Interpretation of Literary Texts," *New Literary History* 11 (1979–80):451–67.

15. William Carlos Williams, *I Wanted To Write a Poem*, ed. Edith Heal (Boston: Beacon, 1958), p. 49.

16. William Carlos Williams, "A Beginning on the Short Story," in *The Selected Essays of William Carlos Williams* (New York: Random House, 1954), 119 (italics mine) (hereafter cited parenthetically in the text).

17. Meridel Le Sueur, Preface to *Women on the Breadlines* (Minneapolis: West End Press, 1984), n.p.

18. Meridel Le Sueur, *The Girl* (Minneapolis: West End Press, and MEP Publications, 1982), 68.

19. Jane Tompkins, *Sensational Designs, The Cultural Work of American Fiction, 1790–1860* (New York: Oxford University Press, 1985).

20. Faulkner, *Lion in the Garden*, 18.

21. William Faulkner, *Light in August* (New York: Random House, 1932), 431.

22. William Faulkner, *Absalom, Absalom!* (New York: Vintage, 1936), 191.

23. Richard Wright, *Native Son* (New York: New American Library, 1940), 108–9 (hereafter cited parenthetically in the text).

CHAPTER 7

1. Albert Van Nostrand, *Everyman His Own Poet* (New York: McGraw-Hill, 1968).

2. James Agee and Walker Evans, *Let Us Now Praise Famous Men* (Boston: Houghton Mifflin, 1941), 123–24 (hereafter cited parenthetically in the text).

3. Eric Homberger, "United States," in *The Second World War in Fiction*, ed. Holger Klein, with John Flower and Eric Homberger (London: Macmillan, 1984), 174. For a different, feminist view of the fiction of this war, see Susan Gubar, " 'This Is My Rifle, This Is My Gun': World War II

and the Blitz on Women," in *Behind the Lines: Gender and the Two World Wars*, ed. Margaret Randolph Higonnet et al. (New Haven, Conn.: Yale University Press, 1987), 227–59.

4. Martha Gellhorn, *A Stricken Field* (New York: Penguin, 1986), 249.

5. Kay Boyle, "Decision," in her *Three Short Novels* (Boston: Beacon Press, 1958), 249–50.

6. Harry Brown, *A Walk in the Sun* (New York: New American Library, 1944), 141 (hereafter cited parenthetically in the text).

7. Carlos Bulosan, *America Is in the Heart* (New York: Harcourt, Brace, 1946), 326.

8. T. S. Eliot, "Burnt Norton," in *Chief Modern Poets of England and America* 2:296.

9. Chester Himes, *If He Hollers Let Him Go* (New York: Thunder's Mouth Press, 1986), 14.

10. Gwendolyn Brooks, *A Street in Bronzeville*, in *Blacks* (Chicago: David Company, 1987), 20.

11. Chester E. Eisinger, *Fiction of the Forties* (Chicago: University of Chicago Press, 1963), 234.

Bibliography

Primary Works

Please note that this listing is limited to *novels* by the respective writers, even though many of them included here published many other books. In rare cases, collections of short fiction are also mentioned; these titles have been important to the writer's reputation as novelist.

Agee, James. *Let Us Now Praise Famous Men*. Boston: Houghton Mifflin, 1941.
———. *The Morning Watch*. Boston: Houghton Mifflin, 1951.
———. *A Death in the Family*. New York: McDowell, Obolensky, 1957.
Anderson, Sherwood. *Windy McPherson's Son*. New York: Lane, 1916.
———. *Marching Men*. New York: Lane, 1917.
———. *Winesburg, Ohio: A Group of Tales of Ohio Small Town Life*. New York: Huebsch, 1919.
———. *Poor White*. New York: Huebsch, 1920.
———. *Many Marriages*. New York: Huebsch, 1923.
———. *Dark Laughter*. New York: Boni & Liveright, 1925.
———. *Beyond Desire*. New York: Liveright, 1932.
———. *Kit Brandon: A Portrait*. New York: Scribners, 1936.
Barnes, Djuna. *A Book*. New York: Boni & Liveright, 1923.
———. *Ladies Almanack*. Paris: privately published, 1928.
———. *Ryder*. New York: Liveright, 1928.
———. *Nightwood*. New York: Harcourt, Brace, 1937.
———. *The Antiphon*. New York: Farrar, Straus & Cudahy, 1958.
———. *Spillway*. New York: Harper & Row, 1972.
Bontemps, Arna. *God Sends Sunday*. New York: Harcourt, Brace, 1931.
———. *Black Thunder*. New York: Macmillan, 1935.
———. *Drums at Dusk*. New York: Macmillan, 1939.
———. With Jack Conroy. *They Seek a City*. Garden City, N.Y.: Doubleday & Doran, 1945; republished as *Anyplace But Here*, New York: Hill & Wang, 1966.
Boyle, Kay. *Plagued by the Nightingale*. New York: Cape & Smith, 1931.
———. *Year Before Last*. New York: Harrison Smith, 1932.
———. *Gentlemen, I Address You Privately*. New York: Smith & Haas, 1933.
———. *My Next Bride*. New York: Harcourt, Brace, 1934.

———. *Death of a Man*. New York: Harcourt, Brace, 1936.

———. *Monday Night*. New York: Harcourt, Brace, 1938.

———. *Primer for Combat*. New York: Simon & Schuster, 1942.

———. *Avalanche*. New York: Simon & Schuster, 1944.

———. *A Frenchman Must Die*. New York: Simon & Schuster, 1946.

———. *1939, a Novel*. New York: Simon & Schuster, 1948.

———. *His Human Majesty*. New York: Whittlesey House/McGraw-Hill, 1949.

———. *The Seagull on the Step*. New York: Knopf, 1955.

———. *Generation without Farewell*. New York: Knopf, 1960.

———. *The Underground Woman*. Garden City, N.Y.: Doubleday, 1975.

Cahan, Abraham. *Yekl: A Tale of the New York Ghetto*. New York: Appleton, 1896.

———. *The Rise of David Levinsky*. New York: Harper, 1917.

Cather, Willa. *Alexander's Bridge*. Boston: Houghton Mifflin, 1912.

———. *O Pioneers!*. Boston: Houghton Mifflin, 1913.

———. *The Song of the Lark*. Boston: Houghton Mifflin, 1915.

———. *My Ántonia*. Boston: Houghton Mifflin, 1918.

———. *One of Ours*. New York: Knopf, 1922.

———. *A Lost Lady*. New York: Knopf, 1923.

———. *The Professor's House*. New York: Knopf, 1925.

———. *My Mortal Enemy*. New York: Knopf, 1926.

———. *Death Comes for the Archbishop*. New York: Knopf, 1927.

———. *Shadows on the Rock*. New York: Knopf, 1931.

———. *Lucy Gayheart*. New York: Knopf, 1935.

———. *Sapphira and the Slave Girl*. New York: Knopf, 1940.

Chopin, Kate. *The Awakening*. New York: Herbert S. Stone, 1899.

cummings, e. e. *The Enormous Room*. New York: Boni & Liveright, 1922.

Dargan, Olive Tilford ("Fielding Burke"). *Call Home the Heart*. New York: Longmans, Green, 1932.

———. *A Stone Came Rolling*. New York: Longmans, Green, 1935.

———. As Olive Dargan. *From My Highest Hill*. Philadelphia: J. B. Lippincott, 1941. Expansion of *Highland Annals*. New York: Scribners, 1925.

———. As Olive Dargan. *Sons of the Stranger*. New York: Longmans, Green, 1947.

———. As Olive Dargan. *Spotted Hawk*. Winston-Salem, N.C.: J. F. Blair, 1958.

Di Donato, Pietro. *Christ in Concrete*. Indianapolis, Ind.: Bobbs-Merrill, 1939.

———. *This Woman*. New York: Ballantine, 1959.

———. *Three Circles of Light*. New York: Messner, 1960.

Dos Passos, John. *One Man's Initiation—1917*. New York: Doran, 1920.

———. *Three Soldiers*. New York: Doran, 1921.

———. *Streets of Night*. New York: Doran, 1923.

———. *Manhattan Transfer*. New York: Harper, 1925.

———. *The 42nd Parallel*. New York: Harper, 1930.

———. *1919*. New York: Harcourt, Brace, 1932.

————. *The Big Money*. New York: Harcourt, Brace, 1936.

————. *U.S.A.* New York: Harcourt, Brace, 1938.

————. *Adventures of a Young Man*. New York: Harcourt, Brace, 1939.

————. *Number One*. Boston: Houghton Mifflin, 1943.

————. *The Grand Design*. Boston: Houghton Mifflin, 1949.

————. *Chosen Country*. Boston: Houghton Mifflin, 1951.

————. *District of Columbia*. Boston: Houghton Mifflin, 1952.

————. *Most Likely to Succeed*. New York: Prentice-Hall, 1954.

————. *Midcentury*. Boston: Houghton Mifflin, 1961.

————. *Century's Ebb: The Thirteenth Chronicle*. Boston: Gambit, 1975.

Dreiser, Theodore. *Sister Carrie*. New York: Doubleday, Page, 1900.

————. *Jennie Gerhardt*. New York: Harper, 1911.

————. *The Financier*. New York: Harper, 1912.

————. *The Titan*. New York: Lane, 1914.

————. *The "Genius."* New York: Lane, 1915.

————. *An American Tragedy*. New York: Boni & Liveright, 1925.

————. *The Bulwark*. Garden City, N.Y.: Doubleday, 1947.

————. *The Stoic*. Garden City, N.Y.: Doubleday, 1947.

Du Bois, W. E. B. *The Quest of the Silver Fleece*. Chicago: A. C. McClurg, 1911.

————. *Dark Princess: A Romance*. New York: Harcourt, Brace, 1928.

————. *The Black Flame: The Ordeal of Mansart*. New York: Mainstream, 1957; *Mansart Builds a School*, 1959; *Worlds of Color*, 1961.

Farrell, James T. *Young Lonigan*. New York: Vanguard, 1932.

————. *Gas-House McGinty*. New York: Vanguard, 1933.

————. *The Young Manhood of Studs Lonigan*. New York: Vanguard, 1934.

————. *Judgment Day*. New York: Vanguard, 1935.

————. *Studs Lonigan: A Trilogy*. New York: Vanguard, 1935.

————. *A World I Never Made*. New York: Vanguard, 1936.

————. *No Star Is Lost*. New York: Vanguard, 1938.

————. *Father and Son*. New York: Vanguard, 1940.

————. *Ellen Rogers*. New York: Vanguard, 1941.

————. *My Days of Anger*. New York: Vanguard, 1943.

————. *Bernard Clare*. New York: Vanguard, 1946.

————. *The Road Between*. New York: Vanguard, 1949.

————. *Yet Other Waters*. New York: Vanguard, 1952.

————. *The Face of Time*. New York: Vanguard, 1953.

————. *Boarding House Blues*. New York: Paperback Library, 1961.

————. *Sound of a City*. New York: Paperback Library, 1962.

————. *The Silence of History*. Garden City, N.Y.: Doubleday, 1963.

————. *Lonely for the Future*. Garden City, N.Y.: Doubleday, 1966.

————. *New Year's Eve/1929*. New York: Smith/Horizon Press, 1967.

————. *A Brand New Life*. Garden City, N.Y.: Doubleday, 1968.

————. *Judith*. Athens, Ohio: Duane Schneider Press, 1969.

————. *The Dunne Family*. Garden City, N.Y.: Doubleday, 1976.

————. *The Death of Nora Ryan*. Garden City, N.Y.: Doubleday, 1978.

Faulkner, William. *Soldiers' Pay*. New York: Boni & Liveright, 1926.

————. *Mosquitoes*. New York: Boni & Liveright, 1927.

————. *Sartoris*. New York: Harcourt, Brace, 1929.

————. *The Sound and the Fury*. New York: Cape & Smith, 1929.

————. *As I Lay Dying*. New York: Cape & Smith, 1930.

————. *Sanctuary*. New York: Cape & Smith, 1931.

————. *Light in August*. New York: Smith & Haas, 1932.

————. *Pylon*. New York: Smith & Haas, 1935.

————. *Absalom, Absalom!* New York: Random House, 1936.

————. *The Unvanquished*. New York: Random House, 1938.

————. *The Wild Palms*. New York: Random House, 1939.

————. *The Hamlet*. New York: Random House, 1940.

————. *Go Down, Moses and Other Stories*. New York: Random House, 1942.

————. *Intruder in the Dust*. New York: Random House, 1948.

————. *Requiem for a Nun*. New York: Random House, 1951.

————. *A Fable*. New York: Random House, 1954.

————. *The Town*. New York: Random House, 1957.

————. *The Mansion*. New York: Random House, 1959.

————. *The Reivers*. New York: Random House, 1962.

Fauset, Jessie Redmon. *There Is Confusion*. New York: Boni & Liveright, 1924.

————. *Plum Bun*. New York: Stokes, 1929.

————. *The Chinaberry Tree; A Novel of American Life*. New York: Stokes, 1931.

————. *Comedy, American Style*. New York: Stokes, 1933.

Fitzgerald, F. Scott. *This Side of Paradise*. New York: Scribner's, 1920.

————. *The Beautiful and Damned*. New York: Scribner's, 1922.

————. *The Great Gatsby*. New York: Scribner's, 1925.

————. *Tender Is the Night*. New York: Scribner's, 1934.

————. *The Last Tycoon*, ed. Edmund Wilson. New York: Scribner's, 1941.

Fitzgerald, Zelda. *Save Me the Waltz*. New York: Scribner's, 1932.

Glasgow, Ellen. *The Descendant*. New York: Harper & Brothers, 1897.

————. *Phases of an Inferior Planet*. New York: Harper & Brothers, 1898.

————. *The Voice of the People*. New York: Doubleday, 1900.

————. *The Battle-Ground*. New York: Doubleday, 1902.

————. *The Deliverance*. New York: Doubleday, 1904.

————. *The Wheel of Life*. New York: Doubleday, 1906.

————. *The Ancient Law*. New York: Doubleday, 1908.

————. *The Romance of a Plain Man*. New York: Macmillan, 1909.

————. *The Miller of Old Church*. New York: Doubleday, 1911.

————. *Virginia*. New York: Doubleday, 1913.

————. *Life and Gabriella*. Garden City, N.Y.: Doubleday, 1916.

————. *The Builders*. Garden City, N.Y.: Doubleday, 1919.

————. *One Man in His Time*. Garden City, N.Y.: Doubleday, 1922.

————. *Barren Ground*. Garden City, N.Y.: Grosset and Dunlap, 1925.

————. *The Romantic Comedians*. Garden City, N.Y.: Doubleday, 1926.

————. *They Stooped to Folly*. Garden City, N.Y.: Doubleday, 1929.

————. *The Sheltered Life*. Garden City, N.Y.: Doubleday, 1932.

———. *Vein of Iron*. New York: Harcourt, Brace & Co., 1935.
———. *In This Our Life*. New York: New York: Harcourt, Brace & Co., 1951.
———. *Beyond Defeat: An Epilogue to an Era*, ed. Luther Y. Gore, Charlottesville: University Press of Virginia, 1966.
Gordon, Caroline. *Penhally*. New York: Scribner's, 1931.
———. *Aleck Maury, Sportsman*. New York: Scribner's, 1934.
———. *The Garden of Adonis*. New York: Scribner's, 1937.
———. *None Shall Look Back*. New York: Scribner's, 1937.
———. *Green Centuries*. New York: Scribner's, 1941.
———. *The Women on the Porch*. New York: Scribner's, 1944.
———. *The Strange Children*. New York: Scribner's, 1951.
———. *The Malefactors*. New York: Harcourt, Brace, 1956.
———. *The Glory of Hera*. Garden City, N.Y.: Doubleday, 1972.
H.D. (Hilda Doolittle). *Palimpsest*. Paris: Contact Editions, 1926.
———. *Hedylus*. Boston: Houghton Mifflin, 1928.
———. *Kora and Ka*. Dijon: Imprimerie Darantiere, 1934.
———. *The Usual Star*. Dijon: Imprimerie Darantiere, 1934.
———. *Nights*. Dijon: Imprimerie Darantiere, 1935.
———. *The Hedgehog*. London: Brendin, 1936.
———. *Bid Me to Live (A Madrigal)*. New York: Grove Press, 1960.
———. *HERmione*. New York: New Directions, 1980.
———. *Nights* (John Helforth). New York: New Directions, 1986.
Hemingway, Ernest. *In Our Time*. New York: Boni & Liveright, 1925.
———. *The Torrents of Spring*. New York: Scribner's, 1926.
———. *The Sun Also Rises*. New York: Scribner's, 1926.
———. *A Farewell to Arms*. New York: Scribner's, 1929.
———. *To Have and Have Not*. New York: Scribner's, 1937.
———. *For Whom the Bell Tolls*. New York: Scribner's, 1940.
———. *Across the River and into the Trees*. New York: Scribner's, 1950.
———. *The Old Man and the Sea*. New York: Scribner's, 1952.
———. *A Moveable Feast*. New York: Scribner's, 1964.
———. *Islands in the Stream*. New York: Scribner's, 1970.
———. *The Garden of Eden*. New York: Scribner's, 1986.
Herbst, Josephine. *Nothing Is Sacred*. New York: Coward-McCann, 1928.
———. *Money For Love*. New York: Coward-McCann, 1929.
———. *Pity Is Not Enough*. New York: Harcourt, Brace, 1933.
———. *The Executioner Waits*. New York: Harcourt, Brace, 1934.
———. *Rope of Gold*. New York: Harcourt, Brace, 1939.
———. *Satan's Sergeants*. New York: Scribner's, 1941.
———. *Somewhere the Tempest Fell*. New York: Scribner's, 1947.
———. *New Green World*. New York: Hastings House, 1954.
Hughes, Langston. *Not without Laughter*. New York: Knopf, 1930.
———. *Tambourines to Glory*. New York: Day, 1958.
Hurston, Zora Neale. *Jonah's Gourd Vine*. Philadelphia: J. B. Lippincott, 1934.
———. *Their Eyes Were Watching God*. Philadelphia: J. B. Lippincott, 1937.

————. *Moses, Man of the Mountain*. Philadelphia: J. B. Lippincott, 1939.
————. *Seraph on the Suwanee*. New York: Charles Scribner's Sons, 1948.
La Farge, Oliver. *Laughing Boy*. Boston: Houghton Mifflin, 1929.
————. *Sparks Fly Upward*. Boston: Houghton Mifflin, 1931.
————. *The Enemy Gods*. Boston: Houghton Mifflin, 1937.
————. *The Copper Pot*. Boston: Houghton Mifflin, 1942.
Larsen, Nella. *Quicksand*. New York: Knopf, 1928.
————. *Passing*. New York: Knopf, 1929.
Le Sueur, Meridel. *The Girl* (from fiction published from 1935 to 1945).
    Minneapolis, Minn.: West End Press, 1978.
Lewis, Sinclair. *Our Mr. Wrenn*. New York: Harper, 1914.
————. *The Trail of the Hawk*. New York: Harper, 1915.
————. *The Job*. New York: Harper, 1917.
————. *The Innocents*. New York: Harper, 1918.
————. *Free Air*. New York: Harcourt, Brace & Howe, 1919.
————. *Main Street*. New York: Harcourt, Brace & Howe, 1920.
————. *Babbitt*. New York: Harcourt, Brace, 1922.
————. *Arrowsmith*. New York: Harcourt, Brace, 1925.
————. *Mantrap*. New York: Harcourt, Brace, 1926.
————. *Elmer Gantry*. New York: Harcourt, Brace, 1927.
————. *The Man Who Knew Coolidge*. New York: Harcourt, Brace, 1928.
————. *Dodsworth*. New York: Harcourt, Brace, 1929.
————. *Ann Vickers*. Garden City, N.Y.: Doubleday, Doran, 1933.
————. *Work of Art*. Garden City, N.Y.: Doubleday, Doran, 1934.
————. *It Can't Happen Here*. Garden City, N.Y.: Doubleday, Doran, 1935.
————. *The Prodigal Parents*. Garden City, N.Y.: Doubleday, Doran, 1938.
————. *Bethel Merriday*. Garden City, N.Y.: Doubleday, Doran, 1940.
————. *Gideon Planish*. New York: Random House, 1943.
————. *Cass Timberlane*. New York: Random House, 1945.
————. *Kingsblood Royal*. New York: Random House, 1947.
————. *The God-Seeker*. New York: Random House, 1949.
————. *World So Wide*. New York: Random House, 1951.
McCullers, Carson. *The Heart Is a Lonely Hunter*. Boston: Houghton Mifflin,
    1940.
————. *Reflections in a Golden Eye*. Boston: Houghton Mifflin, 1941.
————. *The Member of the Wedding*. Boston: Houghton Mifflin, 1946.
————. *The Ballad of the Sad Café and Other Works*. Boston: Houghton Mifflin, 1951.
————. *Clock without Hands*. Boston: Houghton Mifflin, 1961.
McKay, Claude. *Home to Harlem*. New York: Harper & Brothers, 1928.
————. *Banjo*. New York: Harper, 1929.
————. *Gingertown*. New York: Harper, 1932.
————. *Banana Bottom*. New York: Harper, 1933.
Porter, Katherine Anne. *Flowering Judas*. New York: Harcourt, Brace, 1930.
————. *Pale Horse, Pale Rider*. New York: Harcourt, Brace, 1939.
————. *Ship of Fools*. Boston: Atlantic Monthly Press, 1962.

Roth, Henry. *Call It Sleep*. New York: Ballou, 1934.
Stein, Gertrude. *Three Lives*. New York: Grafton Press, 1909.
———. *The Making of Americans*. Paris: Contact Editions, 1925.
———. *Ida a Novel*. New York: Random House, 1941.
———. *Brewsie and Willie*. New York: Random House, 1945.
———. *Mrs. Reynolds and Five Earlier Novelettes*. New Haven, Conn.: Yale University Press, 1952.
———. *A Novel of Thank You*. New Haven, Conn.: Yale University Press, 1958.
———. *Fernhurst, Q.E.D., and Other Early Writings*. New York: Liveright, 1971.
Steinbeck, John. *To a God Unknown*. New York: Ballou, 1933.
———. *Tortilla Flat*. New York: Covici Friede, 1935.
———. *In Dubious Battle*. New York: Covici Friede, 1936.
———. *Of Mice and Men*. New York: Covici Friede, 1937.
———. *The Grapes of Wrath*. New York: Viking, 1939.
———. *The Moon Is Down*. New York: Viking, 1942.
———. *Cannery Row*. New York: Viking, 1945.
———. *The Wayward Bus*. New York: Viking, 1947.
———. *The Pearl*. New York: Viking: 1947.
———. *East of Eden*. New York: Viking, 1952.
———. *Sweet Thursday*. New York: Viking, 1954.
———. *The Short Reign of Pippin IV: A Fabrication*. New York: Viking, 1957.
———. *The Winter of Our Discontent*. New York: Viking, 1961.
Toomer, Jean. *Cane*. New York: Boni & Liveright, 1923.
Welty, Eudora. *The Robber Bridegroom*. New York: Doubleday, Doran, 1942.
———. *Delta Wedding*. New York: Harcourt, Brace, 1946.
———. *The Golden Apples*. New York: Harcourt, Brace, 1949.
———. *The Ponder Heart*. New York: Harcourt, Brace, 1949.
———. *Losing Battles*. New York: Random House, 1970.
———. *The Optimist's Daughter*. New York: Random House, 1972.
West, Dorothy. *The Living Is Easy*. Boston: Houghton Mifflin, 1948.
West, Nathanael (Nathan Weinstein). *The Dream Life of Balso Snell*. Paris: Contact Editions, 1931.
———. *Miss Lonelyhearts*. New York: Liveright, 1933.
———. *A Cool Million: The Dismantling of Lemuel Pitkin*. New York: Covici Friede, 1934.
———. *The Day of the Locust*. New York: Random House, 1939.
Wharton, Edith. *The Touchstone*. New York: Scribner's, 1900.
———. *The Valley of Decision*. 2 vols. New York: Scribner's, 1902.
———. *Sanctuary*. New York: Scribner's 1903.
———. *The House of Mirth*. New York: Scribner's, 1905.
———. *The Fruit of the Tree*. New York: Scribner's, 1907.
———. *Madame de Treymes*. New York: Scribner's, 1907.
———. *Ethan Frome*. New York: Scribner's, 1911.
———. *The Reef*. New York: Appleton, 1912.

————. *The Custom of the Country.* New York: Scribner's, 1913.

————. "Bunner Sisters," *Xingu and Other Stories.* New York: Scribner's, 1916.

————. *Summer.* New York: Appleton, 1917.

————. *The Marne.* New York: Appleton, 1918.

————. *The Age of Innocence.* New York: Appleton, 1920.

————. *The Glimpses of the Moon.* New York: Appleton, 1922.

————. *A Son at the Front.* New York: Scribner's, 1923.

————. *Old New York: False Dawn, The Old Maid, The Spark, New Year's Day.* New York: Appleton, 1924.

————. *The Mother's Recompense.* New York: Appleton, 1925.

————. *Twilight Sleep.* New York: Appleton, 1927.

————. *The Children.* New York: Appleton, 1928.

————. *Hudson River Bracketed.* New York: Appleton, 1929.

————. *The Gods Arrive.* New York: Appleton, 1932.

————. *The Buccaneers.* New York: Appleton-Century, 1938.

Williams, William Carlos. *The Great American Novel.* Paris: Three Mountains Press, 1923.

————. *A Voyage to Pagany.* New York: Macaulay, 1928.

————. *White Mule.* Norfolk, Conn.: New Directions, 1937.

————. *In the Money.* Norfolk, Conn.: New Directions, 1940.

————. *The Build Up.* New York: Random House, 1952.

Wolfe, Thomas. *Look Homeward, Angel.* New York: Charles Scribner's Sons, 1929.

————. *Of Time and the River.* New York: Charles Scribner's Sons, 1935.

————. *The Web and the Rock.* New York: Harper & Brothers, 1939.

————. *You Can't Go Home Again.* New York: Harper & Brothers, 1940.

————. *The Hills Beyond.* New York: Harper & Brothers, 1941.

Wright, Richard. *Uncle Tom's Children: Four Novellas.* New York: Harper, 1938.

————. *Native Son.* New York: Harper, 1940.

————. *The Outsider.* New York: Harper, 1953.

————. *Savage Holiday.* New York: Avon, 1954.

————. *The Long Dream.* New York: Doubleday, 1958.

————. *Lawd Today.* New York: Walker, 1963.

Wylie, Elinor. *Jennifer Lorn: A Sedate Extravaganza.* New York: Doran, 1923.

————. *The Venetian Glass Nephew.* New York: Doran, 1925.

————. *The Orphan Angel.* New York: Knopf, 1926.

————. *Mr. Hound and Mr. Hazard.* New York: Knopf, 1928.

Secondary Works

This listing is of background and theoretical works; criticism on individual authors and their works can be found in the authors' respective reference guides, in *American Literary Scholarship, an Annual,* published each year by Duke University Press, and such collections of bibliographical essays as *Sixteen Modern American Authors,* ed. Jackson Bryer (Durham, N.C.: Duke University Press, 1973).

Aaron, Daniel. *Writers on the Left.* New York: Harcourt, Brace and World, 1961.

Baker, Houston A., Jr. *The Journey Back: Issues in Black Literature and Criticism.* Chicago: University of Chicago Press, 1980.

Baym, Nina. "Melodramas of Beset Manhood: How Theories of American Fiction Exclude Women Authors." *American Quarterly* 33, no. 2 (Summer 1981):123–49.

Bell, Bernard W. *The Afro-American Novel and Its Tradition.* Amherst: University of Massachusetts Press, 1987.

Benstock, Shari, ed. *Feminist Issues in Literary Scholarship.* Bloomington: Indiana University Press, 1987.

———. *Women of the Left Bank, Paris, 1900–1940.* Austin: University of Texas Press, 1986.

Bridgman, Richard. *The Colloquial Style in America.* New York: Oxford University Press, 1966.

Callahan, John F. *In the African-American Grain: The Pursuit of Voice in Twentieth Century Literature.* Urbana: University of Illinois Press, 1987.

Christian, Barbara. *Black Women Novelists: The Development of a Tradition, 1892–1976.* Westport, Conn.: Greenwood, 1980.

Conder, John J. *Naturalism in American Fiction: The Classic Phase.* Lexington: University Press of Kentucky, 1984.

Cowley, Malcolm. *And I Worked at the Writer's Trade.* New York: Viking Press, 1978.

———. *Exile's Return.* New York: Viking Press, 1951.

———. *A Second Flowering.* New York: Viking Press, 1973.

DuPlessis, Rachel Blau. *Writing beyond the Ending: Narrative Strategies of Twentieth-Century Women Writers.* Bloomington: Indiana University Press, 1985.

Eisinger, Chester E. *Fiction of the Forties.* Chicago: University of Chicago Press, 1963.

Elliott, Emory, ed. *Columbia Literary History of the United States.* New York: Columbia University Press, 1988.

Gates, Henry Louis, Jr. *Black Literature and Literary Theory.* New York: Methuen, 1984.

———. *Figures in Black: Words, Signs, and the Racial Self.* New York: Oxford University Press, 1987.

Gibson, Donald. *Politics of Literary Expression: A Study of Major Black Writers.* Westport, Conn.: Greenwood, 1981.

Gilbert, Sandra M., and Susan Gubar. *No Man's Land: The Place of the Woman Writer in the Twentieth Century.* New Haven, Conn.: Yale University Press, 1988.

Harris, Trudier. *Exorcising Blackness: Historical and Literary Lynching and Burning Rituals.* Bloomington: Indiana University Press, 1984.

Hull, Gloria T., et al. *All the Women Are White, All the Men Are Black, But Some of Us Are Brave.* Old Westbury, N.Y.: Feminist Press, 1981.

Jameson, Fredric. *The Political Unconscious: Narrative as a Socially Symbolic Act.* Ithaca, N.Y.: Cornell University Press, 1981.

Kazin, Alfred. *On Native Grounds.* New York: Harcourt, Brace and World, 1942.

Kenner, Hugh. *A Homemade World: The American Modernist Writers.* New York: Alfred A. Knopf, 1975.

———. *The Pound Era.* Berkeley: University of California Press, 1971.

Kolodny, Annette. "Dancing through the Minefield: Some Observations on the Theory, Practice and Politics of a Feminist Literary Criticism." *Feminist Studies* 6, no. 1 (Spring 1980):1–25.

———. "A Map for Rereading: Or, Gender and the Interpretation of Literary Texts." *New Literary History* 11 (1979–80):451–67.

Kramer, Victor A., ed. *The Harlem Renaissance Re-Examined.* New York: AMS Press, 1988.

Lewis, R. W. B. *The American Adam.* Chicago: University of Chicago Press, 1955.

McCormick, John. *The Middle Distance: A Comparative History of American Imaginative Literature, 1919–1932.* New York: Free Press, 1971.

Newton, Judith, and Deborah Rosenfelt, eds. *Feminist Criticism and Social Change.* New York: Methuen, 1985.

Poirier, Richard. *A World Elsewhere.* New York: Oxford University Press, 1966.

Pratt, Annis. *Archetypal Patterns in Women's Fiction.* Bloomington: Indiana University Press, 1981.

Rideout, Walter. *The Radical Novel in the United States, 1900–1954.* Cambridge, Mass.: Harvard University Press, 1956.

Smith, Henry Nash. *Virgin Land.* Cambridge, Mass.: Harvard University Press, 1950.

Spiegel, Alan. *Fiction and the Camera Eye: Visual Consciousness in Film and in the Modern Novel.* Charlottesville: University Press of Virginia, 1976.

Stepto, Robert B. *From Behind the Veil: A Study of Afro-American Narrative.* Urbana: University of Illinois Press, 1979.

Tomkins, Jane. *Sensational Designs, The Cultural Work of American Fiction, 1790–1860.* New York: Oxford University Press, 1985.

Walcutt, Charles Child. *American Literary Naturalism: A Divided Stream.* Minneapolis: University of Minnesota Press, 1956.

Wilson, Edmund. *Shores of Light: A Literary Chronicle of the Twenties and Thirties.* New York: Farrar, Straus, and Young, 1952.

Index

About the Author

Linda Wagner-Martin, Hanes Professor of English at University of North Carolina, Chapel Hill, is the author or editor of more than twenty-five books. Her *Sylvia Plath, a Biography* has been published in England, Spain, and Germany, as well as in the United States, and her studies of other modern writers—Ernest Hemingway, William Faulkner, William Carlos Williams, Ellen Glasgow, John Dos Passos, Denise Levertov—are widely known. A former editor of the *Centennial Review,* Wagner-Martin taught for twenty years at Michigan State University, where she held various administrative posts as well as taught a range of graduate and undergraduate courses. She has also taught at Wayne State and Bowling Green State universities and has been a Guggenheim fellow, a Bunting Institute fellow, and the recipient of grants from the National Endowment for the Humanities and the American Council of Learned Societies.

The mother of three children, Wagner-Martin is compiling a collection of her essays that focus on women writers, as well as editing essay collections on the poetry of Anne Sexton and Denise Levertov. Her most recent book is *Sylvia Plath: The Critical Heritage* (Routledge and Kegan Paul, 1988).